Conscious Riding is dedicated to the Spiritual Utility Vehicles that plow the soil of our unconscious, transport us to the heights of self-realization and allow us to follow our bliss.

Paul is a lifelong professional living and training horses in Southern Pines, North Carolina. He travels extensively and conducts clinics for Undermountain Farm, The Southlands Foundation, Omega Institute for Holistic Studies, Hunter's Rest, Journeyman Farm, The Low Country Hunt and The Kripalu Center for Yoga and Health.

Consciousriding.com

striberry@earthlink.net   910-692-3729
PO Box 2024 Southern Pines NC 28388

PART I

THE TRAIL TO CONSCIOUS RIDING

OVERCOMING THE FEARS OF FALLING FAILING AND LOOKING FOOLISH

    I was delivered at Manhattan's Flower Hospital via Caesarean section. The sedatives given to Alice allowed me to avoid the rigors of childbirth, but they may have induced my low frustration tolerance and an aversion to new things. I long to return to the Land of Anesthesia but there is no way back. This Is It.

    Otherwise childhood seems agreeable enough, my heroes include the ecstatic Mr. Toad of Toad Hall and the permanently pleasant Winnie the Pooh. On my fourth birthday Dobbin appears, with his glistening eyes and flaring nostrils he looks like The Wishing Horse of OZ. I don't know how he's found his way into my room and I'm not sure I want him stay.

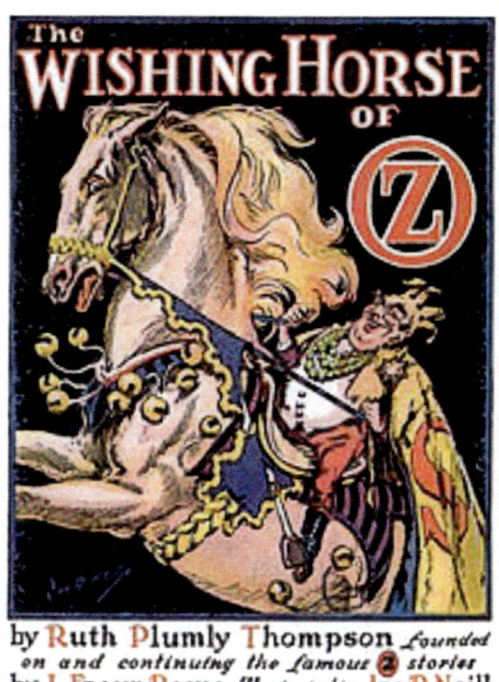

"Get on and give it a try," says William. When that suggestion fails to meet with much enthusiasm, my father picks me up and tries to put me in the saddle but I struggle awkwardly and will have none of it.

Finally, grumbling under his breath he starts the rocking horse in motion and leaves us to get acquainted on our own. I sit with my back against the wall and wait for the horse to stop. The floor is uncomfortable and so is my father's displeasure, but I have to get a rein on my fears of falling, failing and looking foolish before I can deal with Dobbin. That first ride could have been easy — just mount up and go. A yellowing photograph in the family album shows a much smaller steed than the colossus I encountered at the age of four.

Sometime later my mother comes in and repeats Christopher Robin's admonition to a worried Winnie, "always remember you're braver than you believe, stronger than you seem and smarter than you think."

Alice explains that my fears are imaginary just like the creatures in my dreams. Then she climbs on the hobbyhorse and quietly shows me how to rock it back and forth. I watch intently and curiosity takes over. Holding my breath I approach Dobbin slowly, put a tentative hand on his neck and climb cautiously into the saddle. Leaning forward and back I soon become totally absorbed in a world of perpetual motion.

"That's more like it," William returns, happy to find me in the saddle. Overriding my fear produces the attention I crave. I feel noticed, respected and loved. No wonder I become obsessed with horses. Falling had been my greatest fear, but I wasn't falling, failing and or looking foolish… yet.

Each night Dobbin is attached to the bedpost before I say my prayers and go to sleep. My dreams are all about horses and riding which I'm sure is the only desirable life.

My earliest riding lessons come from Western comic books and TV shows. I look forward to Thursday evenings mounted on Dobbin and watching The Lone Ranger on Channel 7. I carefully note how Silver's bridle is adjusted and how the Ranger and Tonto gallop out of town, riding along with them we are certainly safe enough, until I go off my rocker. One evening in my excitement I urge Dobbin along in hot pursuit of Silver and Scout, we are galloping at great speed but when I push Dobbin on - he gets to his tipping point and we crash head over heels on the living room floor.

As I roll over Alice appears "what did you have in mind?" I explain that we were chasing cattle rustlers and my horse fell in a gopher hole. My mother shakes her head as she helps us get upright, "you can't blame this one on Dobbin." She gives me a look that says 'perhaps I am not *always* smarter than I think' and leaves us to watch the rest of the show. I remount and rock on.

Looking back my worries *were* all in my mind. The problem wasn't the hobby horse but rather my doubts and fears in the beginning and excessive exuberance in the end. Anxiety curtails the enjoyment and too much excitement creates disaster.

CAMP SUSQUEHANNA

Adventure calls as I outgrow Dobbin, there are pony rides and wishes for a real horse. Furthermore my parents need a timeout, so I am sent off to Camp Susquehanna in New Milford, Pennsylvania.

The Head Riding Instructor Captain Kirkland was an Officer before the Cavalry changed over from horses to Jeeps and trucks. His fixation with mounted drills went unrequited until he arrived at camp, where his program is all about soldiering on. Riding lessons are not on his radar; he has no time for equitation and maintains that all those instructions would only confuse us. Of course now I don't know what I don't know, but my ignorance really is bliss.

When we ask too many questions, The Captain reminds us "you all learned to walk before you learned to talk and you can learn to ride the same way." His method is trial and error and with enough trials our survival instincts would dictate fewer errors."

Ed Kirkland reminds me of my father – I had to earn his attention and ride to maintain it. One day I ask if my stirrups look even, "How do they feel?" The Captain inquires. His reply turns on a light – learning to feel and solve my own problems would be useful.

His focus is war games, his message "courage is your sword, and winning is the point," we play lots of Capture the Flag and Ringolevio on horseback. When we're not competing he takes us out on long trail rides and calls out 'Prepare To Trot' and then 'Trot – Ho.' Learning to post is a matter of endurance. Cantering comes next and is a great relief after the miles of posting trots.

Another trial and error test is the emergency dismount, jumping off our cantering horses. These dismounts often create the accidents they're supposed to prevent. On my first attempt, I trip and am dragged along until I let go of the reins. The next time my horse is startled and runs off, luckily both feet are out of the stirrups before I hit the ground.

At sunrise we bring the horses in and feed. After our eggs and bacon, we groom, saddle up, and ride all morning. After supper we race down to the barn and the last camper to arrive is thrown in the watering trough. Then the evening is spent attacking the stables with rakes and shovels.

The first Wednesday in July there is a field trip to the livestock auction in Unadilla New York. When we get there most of the kids go off to the refreshment stand for Mountain Dew and Klondike Bars. I make my way down to the corrals to see the horses. I am always kind of a loner looking to escape the noise and carryings-on of the other campers.

I remember the station in Hoboken getting on a crowded camp train. Now I am living in a cabin with eight kids and eating in a mess hall with perhaps 160 others. Susquehanna has round the clock activities and every known sport. The skills of baseball and basketball evade me and football leaves me knocked down and run over. All I want to do is ride, I still remember the camp horses Red Cloud, Adam and Apollo but I can't recall any counselors or my fellow campers. I guess that says it all.

It is quiet down at the holding pens where the horses have been trucked in from out West. Sitting on the top rail of a round corral, I wonder about the horses' stories as they mill around dealing with their neighbors. When a horse is bought to an auction and sold, he has only his instincts to cope with a new job. Will the workload be light or heavy will his rider be kind or oblivious?

Cautiously a small palomino wanders over. I climb down to be on eye level and reach through the rails. At first the mare moves back, I just stand quietly and look away. Eventually she comes forward and lets me rub her neck. For the moment I have her trust and all I can say is 'Golly.'

The auctioneer is starting the bidding and it's time to get back to the group. In about an hour the palomino is ridden in, I catch the Captain's eye, nod my head and quickly look away. He bids two hundred and eighty dollars and the auctioneer calls out "sold." I am a happy camper.

As luck would have it I am assigned to Golly. Dobbin was mostly under control as I rocked along with the Lone Ranger. Now this half broke mare is a real challenge. She is a little hard to get on so I have to be quick. When other horses get too close she lays back her ears and if the warning's not heeded she kicks to signal her displeasure. Constantly vigilant Golly can stop, drop a shoulder and spin all in one motion.

Falling off more than once, I ask the Captain what to do. He just says, "pay more attention." So I begin to notice when I lose Golly's focus and try to bring it back. If she looks at something on the right I turn her left and trot on. When her ears go forward on alert I talk to her and get her listening to me. The Captain is right, "if you maintain attention all is well. When you lose it, you lose it."

Horses are less stressful than people, I am never bored and the work feels like play. On rainy days we sit on hay bales in the Upper Barn and clean old cavalry bridles with Lexol and Brasso. Never one to let a quiet moment to sneak by, the Captain regales us with lectures on self-discipline. "A rider with willpower doesn't sit around and worry. He's on his horse out in front observing the terrain and watching for the enemy."

Our enemies are giant horse flies, ground bees and fire ants, but the Captain doesn't like to see riders looking down. "Look where you're going or you'll go where you're looking." In fact he is right and I hit the ground several times when Golly stops and whirls.

Whether fighting Color Wars or racing on Parents' Weekend, riding is learned in the course of competitions, which push us to our limits. If we are seen falling off, we have to report to the infirmary and explain the accident to the nurse, never a cheerful prospect.

The camp is on a thousand acres and just getting from one activity to the next is a hike. We sleep well in our bunks and look forward to Sunday lunches of pork chops, Bug Juice and chocolate cake. On overnight horseback trips, we use our sleeping bags and ponchos and cook Spam and baked beans in our mess kits. In the middle of the night on picket line duty we drink coffee and refill hay nets while keeping an eye on the horses.

One morning Captain Kirkland announces, "Today we're going to jump."

I am excited. Every November Alice turned me loose at the Madison Square Garden Horseshow. The best class is the International Jumping, where clear rounds are followed by speedy jump-offs. Watching each horse intently, I follow the rhythm cantering to the fences and feel the takeoff. Some of the riders release the reins in the air and others keep the contact and guide their horses early to the next turn.

The Captain makes no mention of instructions but the horsemen are an eager contingent and nobody asks any questions. A truckload of railroad ties has been transformed into a series of jumps on one side of the riding field. The Captain gallops Dionia Dare over the fences for a quick demonstration.

Next a dozen of us line up. "Follow me" is the command as he rides off again. We are heading toward the stables and the horses are happy to move in that direction. Fortunately I am right behind the Captain and Golly likes to keep up, so I just hang on and follow his horse over the fences. Sadly the jumping turns into a great debacle with horses going over, around and stopping in a chaotic cavalry charge.

Once we learn to ride, which means that we survived the first summer, we go on overnight horseback trips, swim the horses in the lake and ride in the Camptown Races, the highlight of Parents' Weekend. The track is set up on the main riding field, outlined with fence posts and giant spools of yellow cord. Parents who had witnessed this spectacle before know to select a spot along the homestretch to enjoy their picnics. Newcomers are left to enjoy lunch on the turns. The races are run flat out, three times around the quarter-mile track. There are the Juveniles for the ponies, Sweepstakes for the fast horses, and Classics for the others. We received one instruction from the Captain: "Ride to win and if your horse is under control, you're not going fast enough."

My plan is to gallop out first and lead to the finish. Since I haven't been schooled in the fine art of race riding, I just take a short hold of the reins and shorten my stirrups trying to look like a jockey. The starter fires a shot and we're off. Golly is in an old hackamore without a bit and the reins feel like they are tied to a tree. But the race is under way and I am out to win the Juveniles.

Once again excessive enthusiasm trumps caution and we're galloping around the turns much too fast. On the final turn heading for the finish line we are out of control, breaking through the yellow strings and racing over picnic blankets. I can still see the alarmed parents and buckets of fried chicken scattering in all directions.

THE FOREST HILLS RIDING STABLES

Summer days with the horses at camp are great, but that still leaves September through June sitting in PS 99 in Kew Gardens. Looking out the classroom window I know early on that I am never going to use long division or the Dewy Decimal System and I am unconcerned with dinosaurs and old wars. My imagination is rounding up horses, but there aren't any in the schoolyard. The one bright spot in class is Katherine Daniels. She has strawberry blonde hair, freckles and smiles whenever I talk to her. We become best friends and she draws the pictures to illustrate my first horse stories.

One day in the fifth grade, the principal – the forbidding Ms. Oliver— enters our room to make an announcement. When she finishes whatever she has to say, she walks right up to me and asks "why aren't you paying attention?"

Without any thought I reply that "I want to be outside" and ask her "if she knows where there are any horses?" The Principal ignores my question, frowns and leaves. Later Katherine tells me about a riding stable in Forest Park, several miles down Union Turnpike.

At the age of eleven my prayers begin and end with asking God for a horse. My father, William The Practical, buys me a bike, points me in the right direction and tells me to 'seek and you shall find.' I ride my Schwinn Traveler down Union Turnpike looking for the horses.

At long last Forest Park comes into view, Eunice appears in the stable yard holding a cup of coffee in one hand and a cigarette and whip in the other. Wanting to make a good impression, I quickly introduce myself and give an account of my riding experience; the emergency dismounts, the fast and furious games and of course the races.

She waves the whip in my direction like The Sorcerer in Fantasia. "You might have talent, but you look like you lack discipline," is her immediate assessment. She then offers to fix whatever needs fixing with a series of lessons. I tell her I don't have any money and she does notice I arrived on a bicycle.

"I had a bike once and we could use some help, Smitty's getting a little long in the tooth to get on some of these horses. Let's see how it goes and maybe you can work for your lessons. We just got this horse in from the track." She brings out Drifter, a tall, skinny Thoroughbred, gives me a quick leg up and leads the horse into the indoor arena. Neither of us had been in an indoor before and I'll never forget my first traumatic lesson.

The would-be school horse just arrived from Belmont where he always raced to the left. I had learned some things at camp but Eunice wanted riding done done her way. "Turn his head, and get that horse on the right lead sit back, heels down… get him under control," the horse is trying to run off and the more I pull on the reins – the faster he goes.

In the midst of my flailing efforts to follow instructions, someone in the hayloft drops a metal ladder down on the cement walkway. When the ladder crashes to the ground, Drifter freezes and bolts Eunice shouts, "Damn it Smitty I told you to lay off the beer." In a flash the horse leaps in the air, reverses direction and races full throttle around the arena.

I cling on for dear life while Eunice yells "stop riding like a monkey on a bicycle!" In this actual emergency I need better instructions. My equitation dissolves, the horse is running away and I'm in survival mode.

My old fears of falling, failing and looking foolish have resurfaced, joined by a new dread - the wrath of Eunice.

Thank God when the horse realizes that the ladder isn't chasing him, he slows down to a walk to catch his breath. I am discouraged more from Eunice's anger than Drifter's performance, as I walk off in the direction of my bicycle, Smitty appears, still holding his bottle of beer. He smiles sheepishly "sorry for causing the skirmish, but don't worry about Eunice's temper. She's always angry that's why I drink."

I thank him and bicycle the five miles home under a cloud. But the net day is a sunny Sunday, I still wan to ride, my spirits revive and it's back to the stables. In spite of or because of the runaway Eunice still thinks I might be useful, so she sends me out to the park on Sargent to learn my way around the bridle path. My job will be taking out one hour trail rides in Forest Park and getting riders back on time and in one piece.

Another challenging assignment is fixing what Eunice calls the *home knockers*; these are the horses that for one reason or another refuse to take their riders down the road, across Union Turnpike and into the Park. These horses will stop, turn around and come trotting back with customers who are never pleased with their abbreviated outings. Eunice and Smitty used to retrain these horses themselves… now it is my turn to turn won't into will.

Smitty grew up on a ranch in Wyoming, worked cattle in Chicago's stockyards and rode rodeo broncs until Mother Nature suggested it was time for another line of work. So he left the circuit, settled down with a barrel racer named Eunice and together they built the stables.

The challenge is getting Drifter out to the park; now he is comfortable in the indoor arena and unwilling to leave. Unlike Captain Kirkland, Smitty believes that instructions are useful. "Always have a clear idea of where you want to go and how you want to get there. When you're dealing with a horse that won't leave increase the pressure. Give him a job, try taking him in the arena and canter in circles. Then give him chance to go out – if he doesn't leave willingly go back and work him again. He must learn the only place he can relax is in the Park. When you get out there let him stand around, then ride him easy around the bridle path. Teach the horse to make predictions, if he goes forward *now* - the rider will lessen the pressure."

I start legging Drifter forward and urging him on but the horse is stopping, I snatch the reins and he starts to go up. "Why is he rearing?"

X"Maybe because you're pulling on him, roughing him up just confirms his worst fears. Punishment doesn't work it interferes with learning. You don't want the horse afraid to fail." Smitty walks around the horse and quietly leads him forward a few steps. "Remind him he's not alone, his trust is the key and always reward the slightest try, let the horse know there's something in it for him."

Well it takes all morning but I do get Drifter into the park. It's really a matter of will and time that overcomes the horse's inertia. Besides I don't have a fall back position. If I want the job I have get the work done. That's the deal.

As the months go by, I heed Smitty's advice and the horses are going well. However Eunice's diet of cigarettes and coffee is taking its toll. She teaches for weeks with the flu and then pneumonia. Finally early Saturday morning, she passes out in the middle of a lesson. I run and get Smitty and we carry her into the house. One of us has to finish the lesson; he opens a beer and sends me back me back to the arena.

"What should I teach them?" I am more inclined to take lessons than give them.

"Teach the riders to *Feel* – give them realistic goals and *focus their attention.* Remember timing is essential because horses have only a few seconds to associate cause and effect. The more precise the timing the more effective the riding."

I thought I'd finish the lesson Eunice was teaching and that would be it. But before the nine o'clock riders get off their horses, the ten o'clock customers are in the ring. It all goes well enough as I try to get them in a feeling mode. The more I watch and the less I say, the quicker they learn.

When riders lose their alignment, they lose their balance and when they lose their balance they lose their control so we work on exercises to steady their legs and keep them aligned. I encourage the students to notice how when their legs come forward they fall back, if the legs go back they fall forward. The goal is self-correction.

People keep arriving for lessons, so I stay in the ring Saturday and all day Sunday and every weekend after that. Sunday evenings I go to the house and give Eunice the cash that accumulates, she always feels better seeing that money on the table.

With Eunice out of the saddle, there are more horses to school and exercise. I start to ride while I am teaching it becomes more like show and tell. When I ask people what they want to learn the classes are more fun. In six weeks Eunice recovers, she still isn't too steady on her feet so I continue to work horses and teach some classes.

TALLY HO
RISK EXERCISE AND EUPHORIA

Eunice is always keen to sell the odd horse, so when Frank Moran is looking for a field hunter to follow the Smithtown Hounds; she decides to sell him Samson. Frank is a big guy, well over six feet tall and needs a sturdy horse. Samson is a Percheron/Thoroughbred cross and a full sized seventeen hands.

What Frank doesn't know is that Samson has no manners to speak of. He runs away with riders in Forest Park and occasionally scrapes them off on the lower branches of mighty maples. Eunice figures he would be less of a liability to Frank than he is to her stable, so she tells him Samson can jump and has hunted. Frank buys Samson for an undisclosed amount, pays a month's board, and says he will send a van for his new horse when he returns from Italy after Thanksgiving.

As Frank drives away, I mention that this was the first I'd heard of Samson's hunting experience. "And how do you know he can jump?"

"How do you know he can't?" Eunice replies. "Besides, he may not have seen hounds yet, but he will have hunted by the time Frank gets back. You're going to hunt Samson."

I was fourteen at the time and the thrill of foxhunting overwhelmed any hesitation a novice rider would have taking a green horse out with hounds. "What do I need to know?"

"Just get on, kick on, and hang on." Eunice never hunted herself but she had been quite a barrel racer. "And I suppose you'll need the right clothes." She gives me three hundred dollars. I take the subway to Miller's in Manhattan. The salesman helps me pick out a new hunt cap, breeches, a black coat, and some secondhand boots that are just my size. If I don't know the script, at least I can look the part.

On the following Thursday, Smitty drives the van out to Long Island, while I pepper him with questions. He allows he'd never actually been foxhunting. "But if I found myself out there, I'd follow some people who knew what they were doing." He finishes by saying that if Samson becomes impossible; I should pull up and come back. He will be waiting at the main house. It all boils down to the same advice Eunice gave me, get on and go.

We pull the van up on the lawn of the biggest house I have ever seen. It is the first formal hunt of the season and there must be a hundred horses ready to go. I comment on the numbers with dismay, but Smitty assures me that "more is better. You won't be noticed quite so much." Samson thinks he's at the circus as he clatters down the ramp. Smitty tightens the girth and tosses me into the saddle before I can ask any more questions. The horse wants to investigate everything all at once, Smitty quietly motions to me to trot him in circles.

The hunt begins with the blessing of the hounds. As the priest gives his benediction, horses and riders stand reverently — all except Samson, who is circling the lawn like a prehistoric bird looking for a place to land. The blessings end, the huntsman blows his horn, and the hounds move off. I work my way into the line behind two friendly, well-dressed ladies who look like they'd hunted before. I quietly tell them this is my first time and it's obvious my horse hadn't done much hunting either.

One of the women points to the safe section, a group of riders called Hilltoppers who follow along and go around the jumps. She suggests I ride with them, but before I have time to turn in that direction, all Hell breaks loose. A red fox jumps out of the bushes and races into the woods. The hounds are in full cry - the huntsman is sounding "Gone Away," on the horn and Samson and I are swept along in the first flight.

"Get a grip, we're on a run," one of the ladies calls out. Samson is amazing, galloping over ditches and jumping stonewalls. The horse is doing everything he can to keep up with the fleeing herd as I cling to his mane to stay on. We run for what seems like the better part of an hour, his Thoroughbred mind wants to go on, but his Percheron body is definitely slowing down.

Finally, Samson breaks to a trot then a walk, sweating and breathing hard. I am still excited as I watch the hunt disappear in the distance, but my enthusiasm wanes as I realize that I am lost in a forest that might go on forever. I think of Smitty, he may never find me in these trees, I imagine Frank Moran losing Samson and picture Eunice refunding the money. Finally I think of myself, better to be lost forever than face the wrath of Eunice.

In the midst of my prayers and trying to cut a deal with God, who shows up but the two nice ladies I'd been with at the start. "My horse lost a shoe," Betsy declares. "And I pulled up to make sure they were okay," Emily adds.

I am about to tell them that I was just asking God for a map, but they can see I am lost. "Fritzy Muller's house isn't far off," Betsy says. "We can call and have the van pick you up."

The ladies are chatting about the horses, the run and the hounds. I ride along quietly, thankful that somebody knows the way back. When we get to Fritzy's house, I hold the horses while the ladies go inside.

A little while later Smitty drives up. "How'd it go?" I tell him about jumping the stonewalls and charging through streams, this is camp on steroids. When I mention that Samson ran out of gas, Smitty laughs.

It's all-good, there just seems to be more to it than get on, kick on and hang on.

A LITTLE EDUCATION
SELF ACTUALIZE AND FOLLOW YOUR BLISS

Back in the real world my parents and Mrs. Everard, Forest Hills High School's guidance counselor, tell me that I should get an education. I'm not sure just how Middlebury is selected but soon I am on my way to New England. I had studied French in high school, but here they are teaching French in French and I can't understand a word. I had done well in biology however I never anticipated dissecting fetal pigs, brains and all. I spend my time in classes looking out the window lucidly dreaming of jumping stonewalls on Samson.

The cold gray Vermont winter makes me dread the dungeons of academia, however the freshman year does have one interesting class, Psychology 101. The course is taught by a visiting Professor Hopkins who had studied with Abraham Maslow at Brooklyn College. I approach the process of Self Actualization from an equestrian perspective and incorporate my own idiosyncrasies in the search for a better quality of life.

<u>BEINGS NEEDS</u>
<u>SELF-ACTUALIZATION</u>
<u>ESTEEM NEEDS</u>
<u>SAFETY NEEDS</u>

PHYSIOLOGICAL NEEDS
DEFICIT NEEDS

William and Alice had supplied food, shelter and safety. However *belonging* and *friendship* were covered by my preferred companions Dobbin and a Teddy Bear. Professor Hopkins points out if we have issues in our early relationships - we may "fixate" on the same set of needs as an adult. Which might account for my lifelong preoccupation with horses and the Teddy Bear on the couch.

The next step to self-actualization is *esteem,* first the need for the respect of others, however I never considered other people's opinions were really any of my business. The second form of esteem is the need for self-respect, which is based on competence, control and proficiency, which for me is fulfilled by working with horses.

Once the esteem needs are reasonably satisfied, we encounter Self-actualization - the always-evolving need for personal growth. For Maslow, a person is continually *becoming* actualized and never remains static. Self-actualized people are comfortable being alone and enjoy an independence from the social need to fit in. I can relate, I have no idea how to fit in, or even where 'in' is.

Best of all, self-actualizers have more peak experiences that make them feel alive and vital. These highs happen when they are completely involved in an activity for its own sake; the ego falls away and time flies.

Professor Hopkins has us read Joseph Campbell's 'A Hero's Journey' and we are encouraged to create our personal recipe for lasting happiness. Campbell's message inspires me - I decide to follow my bliss and trade Vermont's clouds for California sunshine, I know that French and fetal pigs do not equate to happiness. I have to learn what I have to learn and I have to learn it myself.

When I tell my parents that I am not inclined to pursue an education and want to work with horses - they flinch. But I remind them that I had faced the same predicament when the neighborhood kids were playing baseball and basketball; with no skill or interest in these sports I had located the stables in Forest Park and got a job and if I did it once and I could do again.

Joseph Campbell said it best "If you follow your bliss - you put yourself on a track that has been waiting for you. Don't be afraid, and doors will open where you didn't know they existed."

FOXHILL

I always read the Chronicle of the Horse the moment it arrives, its has all the news of horseshows, foxhunting and eventing. However I turn to the classifieds first, since a job with horses would be the best of all possible worlds. Just as the spring semester is winding down I discover an ad for someone to direct a riding program at the Fox Hill Ranch in Greenfield Park New York. I am on the phone and arranging an interview before I can give it any more thought.

Fox Hill is an old Catskill Hotel with a newly built stable, a small indoor ring and plenty of pastures. Ed Trifler the owner wants the newly renovated resort to be all things to all equestrians. Sounds good to me. He asks me about my experience.

I skip over Dobbin and The Lone Ranger and get right to the exciting summers at Camp playing Capture the Flag, jumping and the races. And then without taking a breath I launch into working at the Forest Hill's Riding Academy; guiding trail rides, fixing home knockers and conclude telling him about Samson and foxhunting with the Smithtown Hounds.

Ed has great plans and the place will open in ten days, he is offering a small weekly salary, room and board and there weren't any other replies to his want ad. The job is mine.

There are some thirty horses in the Pasture that Ed bought without trying. A dealer just dropped them off after an auction in New Jersey. I have a little more than a week to sort them out before the Grand Opening on a July 4th Weekend. Tommy and Harry work in the stable and tell me which horses can be caught and other remedial but useful information.

The horses are untried, the saddles and bridles are new and at the moment nothing goes with anything. But by the end of the week I find out which ones can be ridden and fit them with tack. The unbroken and the unsound are sold back at Bunchy's in Metuchen New jersey. We usually bring seven or eight to the sale and come back with five or six.

I had started riding on Unadilla auction horses at Camp and then Eunice got all her stock from Long Island dealers who picked them up from the sales at New Holland in Pennsylvania. There was always an odd lot of ex-racehorses, ex-show horses and various and sundry others that had been cashed in for any number of reasons. What most of them had in common was if I treated them kindly they would return the favor. Smitty taught me to always give the horses a chance and let them know there was something in it for them.

July 4th the guests arrive in droves and they are all were impatient to ride. After the initial shock, I realize there are too many riders to teach at one time and most of them don't want lessons anyway.

I call on all my Susquehanna experience and offer them a game of Capture the White Flag; at least there are plenty of towels around. They are enthusiastic guests and take the game more seriously than their horsemanship. It is kind of a free-for-all but after two hours they are ready for lunch. In the afternoon we have a mock hunt, which starts over a small outside course that Ed had constructed. The first half is a warm up and the stonewalls and logs are set up on the way back toward the stable.

On Sunday we have the races but these don't turn out very well either, some of the horses never get going and others can't be stopped.

Without much feeling for pacing the program I lose several guests and run out of activities before the last morning. Ed saves the day; he produces a dozen practice polo mallets and a large collection of WWII helmets. Polo balls are in short supply and too small to hit, so I rescue volleyball and press it into service. Thus Fox Hill polo is born in the lower pasture. Everyone starts from scratch, neither the horses nor the riders have played polo before and I had only watched it a few times. I decide to be the referee and spend most of the time just trying to avoid the chaos.

Games and the mock hunt worked the best, racing and polo only created carnage. I have a lot to learn but the secret to the program's success is that the resort is on ninety miles from New York City with its eight million inhabitants there is always a steady stream of guests to replace those who fall by the wayside.

I discover the Windy Hollow Hounds in Florida New York and Ed decides we can take riders to hunt with them on occasion. But our horses haven't hunted and our riders are over their heads. So Ed gets a hold of six beagles and I start feeding and riding out with them. Soon some other strays show up and thus we have the Fox Hill Hounds. We start hunting every Saturday and Sunday morning. The beagles chase chipmunks, squirrels, lizards, anything that moves is fair game and the guests are full of praise for whatever sport is produced. Unfortunately there are more egg farms than fox dens in the area and I'm afraid that the chickens soon become the prey of choice.

The resort business kind of depends on the weather and the guest population ebbs and flows. So during the week I work with horses getting them to jump around the course and preparing some of the better ones for sale. With all these horses around we begin to advertise them in the Millbrook papers and make some money, which always comes in handy. As the horses began to sell Ed builds more jumps and enlarges the obstacles on the hunt course.

Early that fall there is a chill in the air and snow flurries. The Farmer's Almanac says we were heading for a cold winter. When I suggest that we can take some horses to Florida Ed goes for the idea.

Alice and William were living in Lake Worth, which turns out to be a mile away from Wellington, the home of Palm Beach Polo and the newly formed Palm Beach Hunt, it seems like a perfect fit.

Ken Adams is the Master and it isn't hard to find his house with its various and sundry stables, kennels and pillared porticos. Ken is curious as I launch into my description of Fox Hill (I did leave out the carnage and the fallen riders). His face brightens when I mention the horses we want to bring to Florida. The Master thinks we might make them available to would-be foxhunters. He suggests if we could hire some out and sell a few we might make some money. Ed would like that and there is a long list of resort guests that might try their luck in in West Palm.

I find a stable on South Shore Drive, Casey Davis is sure we can bring a dozen horses down and board them in her facility. There are plenty of veterinarians, farriers and a Tackeria all in place for the horseshow crowd.

We leave the Catskills in a late October snowstorm, Ed is driving the eight-horse van and I had the four-horse trailer in tow. Somewhere in North Carolina the snow changes to rain and we arrive in Wellington driving straight through in twenty-four hours. The 12 horses are turned out in a large pasture and we take three days to recover.

The Palm Beach Hounds are certainly better organized than the Fox Hill Beagles. They go out on Wednesday afternoons and Saturday Mornings. Most of them are extras from several Virginia hunts, so they enjoy a uniform appearance and had been well trained. Unfortunate their training diminishes over time and in the end they can't resist engaging with armadillos that provide very little sport since their major defense is rolling up in a ball and waiting till the siege is over.

Still I want to learn what I can and volunteer to take hounds with the other whips; this eventually leads to some assisting in the hunt field. Since we are hunting within Wellington's domain the jumps have to be put out on Friday night and picked up after the hunt on Saturday. They were all newly constructed three-foot wooden chicken coops in six foot sections and were definitely on the heavy side which is supposed to prevent horses from knocking them over. One of the volunteers always brings along a case of Budweiser so by the end of the evening some of the jumps end up in spots that are hard to discover while hunting and difficult to locate the next day.

The founding members of the hunt were the wives of some of the polo players. The ladies rightly decided they would enjoy an equestrian activity of their own. Some of the hunts are better than others but all the stirrup cups and breakfasts are outstanding. The Palm Beach Hunt would be acclaimed first and foremost for its hospitality.

Since we were hunting in largely incorporated areas it is sometimes necessary to lay a drag, this line of scent will keep hounds working in the woods and swamps and not running around the Wynn Dixie Parking lot. And after each run we stop and drinks are served by nice people in shiny new trucks who enjoy the thrills and spills with their seat belts fastened. There are glasses of Hunting Port and Sherry before, during and after the hunt, the alcoholics are certainly not anonymous and our Fox Hill guests blend seamlessly into the festivities.

`   As luck would have it we did sell some horse and I had made some money at the end of the season. I drive the horses back to the Ranch and realize if I am going to expand my horizons it is time to move on.

FOXHUNTING

I head west in Volkswagen with a well broken-in saddle and a trunk full of enthusiasm. Luck is as good as skill as long as it lasts, when the money gets low, I manage to find work exercising polo ponies at Willowbend north of Dallas and later riding horses for the Master of the Roaring Creek Hounds in Woody Creek near Aspen. Of course Colorado is cold and it snows all the time so the horses have to be shod with caulks and snowball pads. Some friendly Colorado foxhunters tell me about the West Hills Hunt in the San Fernando Valley where I can find horses, hounds and sunshine. So before the next blizzard, I leave for California.

I arrive in Chatsworth around noon and stop at Bob's Pizza Place for lunch. The slice is hot and the owner cheerful. "I see you're from New York," he says, glancing at my license plates. "What brings you to the Valley?" Another slice appears on another paper plate and I tell him I'm looking for the West Hills Hunt. "The huntsman comes in here once in a while," Bob gives me directions to the kennels.

I find Dave Wendler at the stables on Winnetka Avenue and inquire about a job. Dave smiles and asks if I've ever hunted? I tell him about my day out with Smithtown and add that I like to run and jump.

"Running and jumping is fine while you're keeping up with the hounds. But there is more to it than that." Dave had come to hunting via the rodeo circuit and is very much like Smitty with similar ideas on training. He maintains that horses and hounds learn into softness. "Make sure they know when they get it right. When they feel good about themselves they'll probably do it right again." We talk for a while longer and he decides to give me a chance. The next day I start riding out with hounds for their training and mine.

Dave is quiet with the horses and hounds and always quick to praise them, his well-timed support helps me too. In the course of the summer I learn the hound's names and personalities and can usually tell which one's are really hunting. When the season starts in September, I am whipping-in, turning hounds off deer that they aren't supposed to chase and gathering up the pack for the Huntsman. We are mostly chasing coyotes that are fit and fast from living on rabbits, while the hounds eat kibble in the kennels. Coyotes often wait on a hillside for the hunt to catch up and then lead us on another merry chase. Knowing the countryside they seldom come to grief and I soon realize that they are much safer than the foxhunters.

Diamond Bar is sponsoring a cross-country to advertise their upscale Los Angeles home sites. There is no entry fee, free stabling and plenty of prize money. The hunt season is over, the horses are fit and it sounds like fun. Chrome is my candidate he can usually negotiate all kinds of trappy country. But the course is newly constructed and the going is deep.

NOT EVERY EXPERIMENT IS SUCCESSFUL

Falls happen with I venture beyond the edge of my skill and/or the horses ability. As luck would have it neither horse nor rider were much the worse for wear. We withdrew from the competition and the stewards took the jump out of the course. Dave gave me one of his horses to ride and we came in third in one division or another.

Foxhunting turns out to be a good career move and a great way see the country. There are always ads in the Chronicle of the Horse for hunt staff and riders at private stables. The season lasts from September to March and then I would move on. After West Hills, I whipped in for the Deep Run Hunt near Richmond, Mr. Stewart's Cheshire Hounds in Unionville, and the Los Altos Hunt in Woodside. In the course of my travels I discovered Southern Pines with its warm climate, good footing and friendly inhabitants. My plan is to make and sell some field hunters.

Trying to hunt Mr. Pibbs is an edifying experience. A Holsteiner Thoroughbred cross he was bred in Las Vegas and found himself at Phillip Dutton's stables in Unionville. Apparently the horse was agitated and climbing the walls when Maya saw him in the indoor ring. Pibbs was a natural athlete and had been pushed along at a great rate until his mind was frazzled. Phillip decided at that point the horse was more trouble than he was worth so Maya bought him at a deep discount. Phillip is a world-class Olympic eventer and Maya was long listed for the Canadian team but Pibbs is over the top, he won't stand still and has to be run through the cross-country start box, his dressage is erratic, and he leaves out strides and knocks down rails in the stadium jumping. He went out to clients on trial several times but was always sent back.

After some less than stellar competitions Maya brought the horse to Southern Pines and offered me a test ride on the hunter trial course. The fences were solid and far apart so Pibbs took them in stride and since eventing was no longer his ticket to stardom we thought he might be happier foxhunting. Maya was tired of paying the bills and gave him to me. If all went well I would sell the horse and share the money.

To become a useful field hunter a horse has to stand quietly at the meet, stay in line and keep his distance to avoid getting kicked. Tailgating is out and there must be under control at the fences. If the horse in front refuses or a rider falls off (and it does happen), we don't want to be part of the accident. Another essential is that a horse has to willingly leave the group for one reason or another. Some of the demands are counterintuitive to a horse's normal instincts. In their natural setting horses run in a tightly packed herd and the one that falls behind or wanders off can become lunch for a predator.

Some people ride to hunt, intently watching the hounds and knowing most of them by name. The others hunt to ride; they enjoy the jumps, the traditions and the social aspects. In either case foxhunters need a horse that's ready to stay the course. Pibbs is six years old, jumps with abandon and has more stamina than he knows what to do with.

Our first hunt was the Opening Meet on Thanksgiving. I know it's better to introduce a new horse on Labor Day when the weather is warm, there are fewer riders and the hounds are just out for exercise. But I don't let reality dampen my optimism, after all this is a universe of unlimited potential and you never know without a try. So here we are in Hobby Field with eighty other horses, a Priest blessing forty foxhounds and perhaps five hundred spectators with a variety of drinks.

During the blessing while the others horses were still and their riders reverent, Pibbs exhibits some airs above the ground, this might be our last rites. When the Huntsman sounds his horn and cast the hounds, my horse grabs the bit and charges to the front of the field, he is happy enough to gallop along with the other horses but I know he won't turn or stop. After an eternal ten minutes the hounds check, the other horses come to a halt and we just keep going. As it turns out I am introducing a horse to an occupation for which he might not have an aptitude.

I am over doing it and making the same mistake as his prior owners. My ego had taken the ride and left common sense in at home. I have to take my time and let Pibbs take his. He wasn't delighted with being caught, groomed or saddled, so we have to slow down and work on those things first. In order to train Pibbs I have to first get his attention, earn his trust and let him understand he is in safe hands. He had been moved up too fast in competition and now he is being ridden out in the woods to run around with red-coated riders cracking whips at a pack of carnivores.

I remembered Smitty's advice, "let the horse know there's something in it for him." Catching Pibbs in his pasture is the foundation of a new relationship, rushing makes him nervous, I can't out run him, so the horse has to realize it is safe to come to me. I begin by going down to his paddock and just waiting near a tree till the horse gets curious. There is no halter; just a few carrots and when Pibbs comes around I feed him and rub his neck. After a few days he looks forward to my arrival and lets me slip on his halter as he receives his treats.

The next step is grooming; bring him in, brush him until he relaxes and turn him out again without trying to put on a saddle. I always give him a carrot when I appear and another one when I turn him back out so he doesn't run off. After several days its time to start saddling and leading him around, of course had been groomed and saddled for years but its time for new associations with these basic procedures. I am developing patience and Pibbs is working on trust.

Then it's time for hours of schooling, taking the time to work through the gap between the past where Pibbs had been frazzled and the future about which he is wary. Horses naturally stand around and so we do that for a while, then it's on to bending. We walk and rest time and time again until the horse becomes sensitive to the prospect of slowing down and stopping. We work on halts from the trot and finally from the canter, three weeks later we can down shift and brake. Next we go out and repeat the exercises in the woods.

I take every opportunity to trail ride with others following along, passing and being passed. I ride Pibbs in a full cheek snaffle and then a gag, didn't see much change. When I try a Pelham with a curb chain the horse bounces along like a concrete trampoline. Back to the snaffle I can take a little more hold with a less severe bit and that works best.

The next time we are out with hounds it's on a Tuesday in February, not too many people in the field and thankfully a slow day. I ride him in the back of the Hilltoppers where serpentines and circles won't bother anyone. In the weeks that follow I take him to the back of the second flight. When we're moving on and he goes into overdrive I keep him slightly bent so I can see the corner of his eye. Retrieving his attention when it wanders is the trick that enables me to hunt the horse. Its still rough going in spots but the good days are fun.

Foxhunting is subject to the mysteries of scent. There's always a reason for a blank day, too dry or too wet, too hot or to cold, too early morn or too late in the afternoon. Of course we might have perfect conditions but the fox is on vacation. With Pibbs we're always on the starting line, ready to hunt if the fox shows up or hunting to ride if he doesn't.

OFF TO THE RACES

Flyer is a Master's horse, a big willing Thoroughbred who is always ready to run. He has a long stride and stands well off from the jumps. His lip tattoo indicates he is eight years old and has been on the racetrack. One day after hunting Tommy Mein asks me if I want to ride the horse in the Delmonte Gold Cup. Never one look before I leapt I say "sure." Tommy goes on to explain that the races are run at Pebble Beach, an ocean front conclave of estates surrounded by a 17-mile drive. The feature race is run on the Spy Glass Hill golf course, three and a half times around a one-mile course with a total of twenty-one jumps, most of them brush fences well endowed with timber.

The races were a yearly event and usually included entries from West Hills, Los Altos and Santa Inez hunts. The jockeys were mostly foxhunters that prioritized adrenalin rushes over the risks to their lives and limbs. Conditioning Flyer for the races I receive all kinds of advice. Endurance riders told me to trot the horse for miles to build him up without breaking him down. An ex-jockey suggested wind sprints on hills and galloping to develop his lungs. Dave thought if I just kept hunting him all would be well. Well I did some of everything, miles of trotting, long gallops and lots of hunting. My previous racing had been on Golly at camp and there wasn't any training for the Juveniles.

On the first Saturday in April, I mount Flyer at the stables and ride over to the Spy Glass Hill; there are sailboats out on the ocean and seals barking on the rocks. The jumps range in height from and 3'6'' to 3'9' and are brushed out to twelve feet. Flyer has his head up and is cantering in place. Fortunately there is no time to reconsidered Mr. Mein calls out "Good Luck" and it is on to the start. Tim Durant the Galloping Granddad leans over to give me some instructions. "There are eleven horses in this race, break out in front, avoid the crowd and keep up a good pace." His idea was that the other riders might slow us down. I surveyed the triangular course; I needed to hold it together on the turns, not too wide and no cutting in. He carefully instructed me to steady Flyer on the way to the fences and not to let the

others get ahead of him.

At the start Flyer is inching forward when the starter bell rings, the saddlecloth is number 1 and we break out in front galloping through another lucid dream. I just have to steer and stay with the horse as he inhales the course sailing over the fences. We go a little wide on the first turn and slip hitting some ice plant; we correct and ride for the middle of the track where we will stay for the duration. I can hear Tim urging his horse on toward the end and realize he is running along in my wake.

When we get to the last jump, an oversized Aiken, Tim pulls to the inside, lays his whip on and shoots past me to the finish line. I had been following his instructions to the letter and moving right along. But now it's his race and he's winning. Tim was 76 at the time and I was 36, it's a fact I have been outridden and outsmarted. He had found someone to set the pace and could run care free for the first three miles until it was time to go into overdrive. We were out-foxed, but I am pleased, Flyer is sound and ready to go again, Tommy Mein is delighted with a second.

ON TO IRELAND

Ireland is the Mecca of foxhunting and having sold several horses I think this is an opportune time to make my pilgrimage to Donadea and work for Lady Connolly Carew. Her home is Castletown an impressive estate and the largest mansion in Ireland. Baron Carew tells me the building was the inspiration for our White House in Washington.

There are several fields of homebred horses and my job is conditioning them up and getting them out with hounds. The horses are mostly cooperative; they have been bred to hunt and raised together so they'll usually follow each other along no matter how daunting the challenge. We hunt with the Kildare, the Scarteen and several other packs.

The hardest part of hunting in Ireland for me is getting to meets. I am driving an ancient Minnie-Cooper van everyone calls Captain PugWash and pulling a good-sized Irish hunt horse in a tiny wooden trailer. Of course the steering wheel is on the right and I'm supposed to drive on the left hand side of the road. Driving on the left was originally designed to enable a horseman to carry a sword in his right hand, which was probably more useful for jousting than it is for an American accustomed to interstate highways.

All the speed limits are posted in Kilometers but Captain PugWash is straining to make the hills and we can't go fast enough to break the law. So I am plodding along dreading the next confusing roundabout while deciphering illegible directions.

It seems everyone in the stables was born locally and knows their way around. I have a penchant for disorientation and my sense of direction isn't what it should be. Everyone assumes when I've been somewhere once I can easily get back there again, which is certainly not the case. My questions are always answered by 'oh go on Lad, you'll be ok.'

Perpetually lost I just drive around what looks like hunt country until I catch sight of the horses or hounds then pull off the road and join the fray. The Irish are more like cowboys than the hunters in at home. They like to have a drink, tell a joke and then daringly jump gates, walls, and huge ditches. Making your way from a great muddy bank to another across a canyon-sized ditch with barbwire at the bottom (to keep the cattle contained) is a real test; in the end I leave the negotiations to the horses. They are on their home turf and will get across double banks without too much meddling.

I lived mostly on Shepherd's pie (potatoes and ground sheep swimming in cholesterol), Guinness Stout and Soda Bread. Caring for four horses and hunting five days days a week certainly prevents insomnia. Lady Carew turned her horses out to pasture after the season. With very little money left and no permanent address I depend on finding work, so I call my agent Candace Smith and get a line on a job back in the San Fernando Valley.

SHOW HORSES

Tom Blakiston a well-known horseman in California was leaving for Mexico. He had sold a couple of jumpers to a rider on the Mexican team and was off to collect the rest of his money. As Candace said, he needed somebody to keep things going while he was away. I started to recite my resume but he shook his head.

He has a thoroughbred gelding brought out and gives me a leg up. He lets us warm up for five minutes and has us jump around a course in the main ring. I get the horse in front of my leg and with a bit of over riding make it down the lines, over the fences and around the turns. He seems satisfied enough… later I find out the horse was right off the track.

Tom points out a dozen horses that will need grooming and riding. He wants the place kept clean and in my spare time the jumps could use a coat of paint. He shows me a one-room cabin where I can stay and that is the end of the interview. "Do you want the job?" I did. The next week he is off to Mexico City leaving me with plenty of work. I didn't have much time for a social life, but I could take girls to the movies and a supper of enchiladas at Los Toros.

Five years later I am still living in that cabin and learning how show horses are trained, ridden and sold at Southern Comfort Stables. This was a whole different enterprise from the The West Hills Hunt. It turns out that show horses are where the money is. At the time you could sell a hunt horse for twenty five hundred but show horses started at twenty five thousand.

I am learning the business from the ground up; four rides every morning and three every afternoon. Blakiston had more patience than Eunice; he wants the horses shown to their best advantage and then sold. He talks about quality and demonstrates it in his training. "You don't always get everything you ask from a horse – but the more you ask for the more you get." I am learning to keep them light and ride them forward.

We begin schooling the horses on the flat to get them balanced and listening, and then work them over fences with an eye to the shows. Right off the track most of them were pretty green and trainers like Blakiston generally put their 'assistants' on horses that might damage their body or reputation. When asked why I was riding so many unpredictable horses he allowed, "Anything that doesn't kill you will make you ride better."

He wants to accelerate the horse's learning curve without blowing his mind. "Take your time - but get it done quick." I can still hear his words as he brought out the next horse. The horse shows work the same—learn the course and pay attention. I sort out the elements; control depends on balance and balance depends on alignment, of course maintaining alignment and while riding forward is the challenge.

Blakiston's goal is to find what each horse does best; he says 'there are horses for courses.' The trick is schooling the difficult parts anything from getting an automatic lead change to jumping a big vertical off a tight turn. I have to trust the boss, our horses and myself.

Schooling over fences is a great feeling when I get it right. When I don't, my mentor quietly tells me to 'try it again.' He moves the fences to adjust the horse's stride, and tells me to press on or wait a bit. Just like Smitty, Blakiston never stopped until we got it right. The key was in the approach, getting the horse's attention, lining up with the middle of the fence and gathering enough impulsion. I begin to feel when its right, know when its wrong and understand how to change things.

Southern Comfort makes and sells a lot of show horses. I had reached a certain level of competence hunting and racing now competition requires a more sophisticated ride. The dependable horses with style go to the hunter ring; the ones with more scope enter the jumper classes. This is an exciting business and I am working on the production line, which is constantly producing saleable horses.

NEW GOALS   MORE ATTENTION   BETTER REFLEXES

Riding at the shows is stretching my skills and keeps me moving up. In the jumper classes when I have a clear round and make the jump-off, going against the clock ramps up the pressure. If I push the horse too fast, we'd go wide and lose valuable seconds. Too much speed could cause us to jump from bad spots and hit rails. If I ride too carefully another rider will beat our time. The best rides happened when I don't worry about the clock or the course. With no thoughts of winning or losing, I just look for the next fence, guide the horse and let him jump. Timing, rhythm and balance come together. I get out of my own way and let the horse rise to the occasion.

The customers come at all hours—mornings, afternoons and evenings. The amateurs will buy a green prospect for many times what Blakiston has invested and then they pay to have their horse fed, trained, and shown.

Sometimes they will show the horse themselves, but if they don't win enough, they put it on the market. Blakiston is happy to make the sale for a fee; the client will often buy another horse and start the process over. It was just like Vegas, everyone is buying *hope* and Blackiston has it for sale. I begin to understand his smile whenever he mentions 'money.' He is a good horseman and a shrewd dealer with a sense of humor.

Then one day a mall developer shows up and offers my employer a large bankroll for his twenty acres on Devonshire. Blakiston smiles and takes the offer.

Another job come and gone, so I just kept following my bliss. Kind of like the Lone Ranger; except there isn't a Tonto or a Hiawatha and I wasn't sponsored by Cheerios. As luck would have it reality never overwhelms me, the intervals between jobs were my vacations and there is plenty of travel.

RANCHO SANTA FE
GRAND PRIX JUMPING

Seizing my next opportunity I head for San Diego and begin working at The Riding Club in Rancho Santa Fe. The community is a haven for people who've won at Monopoly, there are tennis courts, surrounded by Golf courses and bridle paths and if all else fails, there's the Del Mar Race Track and La Jolla Beaches.

Tommy Mein had bought Pepper and Chrome as field hunter prospects. They were athletic athletic horses with their own ideas of right and wrong, jumping was all right, but being in close proximity with foxhounds and cracking whips was wrong. The Appaloosa was kicking at everything that moved and the Thoroughbred took off running whenever he heard the horn. My job is finding them a new career.

Twice a week I trailer over to school with Steve and Dianne Grod at Rancho Bernardo. The horses like to jump and Steve always raises the bar to increase their scope. Dianne is well connected with the luminaries of the jumper world and Rodney Jenkins shows up occasionally for West Coast competitions. Watching Rodney school Idle Dice over six foot verticals inspires me to ask more from my horses and myself.

So when a plan is hatched to hold the first California Grand Prix at Rancho Bernardo – we make our entries. I don't know what I was thinking; we are doing some low-level jumper classes but neither the horses nor the rider have shown at this level. I remembered Henry Ford's adage; "If you think you can you probably will – if you think you can't you won't."

Of course I had no health insurance and no one used safe helmets but it's amazing how a little peer pressure moves me along. What I lacked in experience I made up with enthusiasm. I wasn't thinking about winning, actually coming home alive would be half the fun.

The plan is to get Pepper and Chrome ready and able to clear big combinations so we are schooling long lines of four and five-foot fences. This kept the horses attentive and motivated to jump out. The rest of the time it is turning and sprints.

One month later the day arrives. The class is to begin at two in the afternoon but the jumps are set the night before and the course diagram is posted. I am out there studying by dawn's early light. The only thing worse than knockdowns is going off course and since I have lost my way before, I want to etch the course onto my brain. The start is flagged and it looks like crossing the finish line in the time allowed will require some forward riding. The jumps included a bank, the water, and double and triple combinations, eighteen fences in all.

I must have walked the course a dozen times, the footing had been brought in for the show and I noted some soft spots to avoid. Getting around in the time allowed requires particular attention to the critical turns; it's never too early to look where you're going because a good turn can't be abrupt. All of the fences are impressive, so some speed will override the horse's hesitation or my own.

At noon I start to warm up. The schooling area is crowded and the sound of poles being knocked down distracts Pepper. I trot down the hill to the schooling ring at the stables and have my friend Manuel set some fences. I elect not to jump too many, lest I take the edge off, instead I work on turns, cantering concentric circles with decreasing diameters.

Pepper was eleventh and Chrome was sixteenth in the order so I had time to watch other riders negotiate the course and check my initial plan. It looked like the most successful rounds kept moving on at a good rate.

When we are called; we jump some oxers and enter the ring at strong trot. I halt, salute the judge and take full advantage of the one-minute rule to canter a long warm up circle allowing Pepper to see the crowd and the fences.

I collect the horse as we cross the start line and head for the first jump, a brick wall with two rails on top. I move him on for the last three strides; Pepper stands off and clears it with room to spare giving us both a green light. Having walked the course so many times I know it for sure and only have to focus on balance and impulsion.

PEPPER JUMPING IT RIGHT

The next combination is a fair sized oxer with an imposing vertical two strides away. I keep moving up to the spread fence trying to get in close so Pepper won't stand off and take down the back rail. When he jumps it in stride I sit deep, and we jump well over the vertical. There was a triple bar that takes care of itself and then on to the water.

Pepper never liked water that was one of his drawbacks for foxhunting. I know we won't land in the middle - but would he jump it at all? I give the horse a long approach so the water won't surprise him. When his ears perk up and I knew he is focused, sending him on we sail over.

PEPPER DIDN'T LOOK AT THE WATER BUT I DID

My relief is palpable and we finish the course clear and well under the time allowed.

Chrome is only 15.3, but he was up in front and aggressive, I know he will attack the fences. Keeping him attentive and staying with him will be the trick. He can jump anything but often at the last moment and in an unconventional style. My two warm up fences are verticals and I try to get him tightened up on the approach, but this is his first big class and he will do it his way - dropping his less than tidy front legs and powering off his hocks.

When we enter the ring he hardly stops for the salute - I am glad this isn't a dressage test. Chrome is grabbing the bit on our warm up circle instead of looking at the jumps. I am struggling to get his attention so I can steer him around, this will probably be all I can do.

WITH CHROME IT IS HANG ON AND GO

We gallop down to the first fence clear it and run on. Fortunately Chrome is sizing up the fences, when the combinations come up he backs off at the first jump and gives himself a chance to sort out the second or third. When in doubt he over jumps – and all I can do is hang on. We clear the course in the time allowed and Chrome is looking for more challenges as we leave the ring.

I'm afraid my eagerness takes over in the jump off. The pace is a little too fast; we can't reorganize and overshoot the turns. Both horses are strung for the combinations and take down rails in the triple. I know it is rider error, we are out of the ribbons but I am happy with the horses who rose to the occasion.

There is a party at the Clubhouse that night, a pleasant woman hands me a glass of champagne, Sarah Buhler is from Switzerland asks me about Pepper and Chrome. I explain that they belong to a man in Woodside who wants to foxhunt but the horses won't buy it. I knew this was a stretch, but I wanted to see if we could get around the course.

Sarah smiles and asks if I would be interested in going to Switzerland to ride for her brother Marcus. He is in the horse business and wants to sell Swiss

Warmbloods to rich Americans; the assumption is I might have contacts to buy these horses. In reality she probably couldn't find anyone else who would go at the moment. Now I have the Grand Prix Bug and want to ride in Europe.

Pepper and Chrome have done well enough in their first major outing and have some real potential so Dianne will take them and continue their training with an eye to a sale.

SWITZERLAND AND THE HORSE BUSINESS

Two weeks later I arrive at The Hotel Simmenhof in Lenk and am given a room and access to the restaurant that are replete with birchermusli, fondue and chocolate mousse. Marcus Buhler is a Swiss horse dealer who is based at the Simmenhof Stables; I will be riding the Swiss Warmbloods in an indoor arena attached to a hotel.

Buhler is an optimistic horseman with a plan. He buys dressage horses that trained up to third level and above they all perform well on the flat but aren't winning. The theory is that it takes several years to train a dressage horse but we can get them jumping in a week. My job is to reprogram them to jump.

To start the horses Marcus gets on his retired showjumper Gandalf and I am on one of the newbies following along over crossrails and small solid obstacles. This method introduces jumping quickly and works most of the time. There are some clumsy horses that scatter the poles and tip over the boxes, but they are deleted from the program. We are looking for careful horses that like jumping and averse to touching the fences.

Marcus is all about gymnastics, they teach horses to shorten and lengthen their strides and maintain their balance. He carefully watches each horse to see what it does well and what needs improvement. Some horses can stand off and jump but need to collect while others have to move on and stretch. The distance between the fences is set from one to three strides and adjusted to make the horse use his eye and take care of himself.

My job is to ride to the gymnastics at a trot with enough impulsion to jump the first one and then stay on and out of the horse's way. When it works this process improves the horse's confidence. If we make a mistake and crash an oxer, the distances are immediately lengthened and the jumps lowered and to restore the horse's self-reliance. The goal is to jump a big fence off a short stride from a close distance. This requires some presence of mind but it usually works with a supporting leg and hand.

I ride the horses out every few days to give us both some fresh air and a view of the mountains. There aren't many trails nearby, but there are some open fields around the Hotel. The Boden train station is a hundred yards away and the track runs along the edge of the turnouts. Fencing is mostly hot wires and tape, and safety isn't the strong point of this set up.

The plan is to get the horses sold before they get tired of jumping. There are clients coming to look, but I notice the first questions the smart ones ask is "what has the horse done?"

They are jumping around the indoor ring but none of them have competed at the shows. The asking prices are high and without a competition record these clients and their professionals are reluctant to spend a lot of money.

Before long my weekly stipend decreased and the ambiance around the hotel became less welcoming. It seems Herr Buhler wasn't paying his bills and the operation was winding down. The Swiss lady who owned the Simmenhof mentioned that horses could be a great hobby but a second-rate business.

I had never given much thought to money. Wanting to ride and be around the horses, I accepted whatever employers paid as the going rate. Eunice used to buy lunch from time to time. Surely riding and learning from Smitty had been worth my time and effort. Enough was as good as a feast. But now there wasn't enough it is time to move on. I call my agent Candace, she tells me about a job in Mexico and I am on my way.

SOUTH OF THE BORDER
GETTING TO THE END OF MY TETHER

Senor Chedraui and his Family met me in the Airport in Mexico City and we are flown back to Jalapa Vera Cruz. The family Patriarch Lazaro Chedraui had emigrated from Lebanon in 1927 and sold merchandise in a cart on the public square. Today the family owns 183 Super Shopping, Big Box Stores everywhere from Mexicali to the Yucatan.

What do you like to do? Don Antonio asked as we enjoy a Dos Equis in flight.

"I start green thoroughbreds and train them to jump." This is what I had done at Southern Comfort Stable and it is kind of my niche.

"Very well." You could see the wheels turning in Don Antonio's smile. Two days later we fly back to Mexico City have lunch and Senor Chedraui turns me loose at the Hippodrome de las Americas. Since my Spanish is nonexistent, I improvise in French (another romance language) without much success. So it takes me a while to get across the racetrack into the stable area. As luck would have it I meet Enrique a trainer who speaks English. I explain my mission is finding some prospects for Senor Chedraui.

He calls me me Gringo Chedraui and when the other trainers realize that I represent a buyer the stable doors are flung open.

Apparently there is no end of horses for sale. I must have looked at thirty and had them jogged before the races began. I made copious notes on my racing form and certainly didn't want to hurt anyone's feelings even if their horse wasn't particularly sound.

The horses are being saddled for the first race Enrique has to go to the paddock and I find my way back to the rail. This is my first expedition to the track but I have a plan. I picked out a dozen horses that looked like the right type and watched the races all afternoon. I didn't need the winners and I didn't want the horses that came in last. I was looking at the ones that finished in the middle of the field perhaps fourth or fifth.

At the end of the day I had picked out a chestnut mare and a bay gelding. Don Antonio met me at the Clubhouse and we went down to the stable area.

As it turns out Enrique trains for Don Antonio's brother-in-law Senor Fernandez. I point out the two horses I'd selected and they arrive in Jalapa the next day. I named the chestnut mare Senorita and the bay horse Amigo in an effort to demonstrate my new command of the language.

SCHOOLING SENORITA AT HOME

All was well in the beginning at Club Hippico Coapexpan; there we six grooms for fourteen horses and each horse lived in large stall with high ceilings and skylights. When I finish working one horse it is taken to be unsaddled and washed and the next one is tacked up and ready to ride.

Then things change when Senor Chedraui's oldest son Antonio is heading for the Olympic Team. Now it's all about competition he would ride for Mexico in Atlanta and Beijing. The shows were exciting and we did well at first but the more we won the faster Don Antonio would move the horses up in the ranks until they were burning out. Blakiston had wanted horses brought along quietly so he could sell them to amateurs, but in Mexico every class is an effort to make the Team.

When we won everyone was happy. If we lost well the displeasure was palpable. Horses were breaking down and being replaced with an inexhaustible supply of money.

SHOWING SENORITA IN MEXICO CITY

The horses were given intravenous fluids to keep them going in the smog filled altitude of Mexico City and I wasn't thriving in the Zona Rosa. When we got around one course the boss would move them up. You were always over your head and the jumps were getting that way too. We had jumped around well in the morning and then in a bigger class that afternoon my horse caught a pole between his front legs and we somersaulted in a

40

rotational fall. I was lucky to be thrown out of the way. This was the last straw.

TRAINING AMIGO IN JALAPA

My low frustration tolerance began to resurface, I was putting the pressure on the horses and myself and it wasn't working. My moods were fluctuating like the Mexican Stock Market.

I thought back to Psychology 101 and Joseph Campbell. This time my bliss was taking a Uturn. That night I dreamed of Dobbin and remembered that there was no problem we couldn't run away from. I had been in Vera Cruz for two years, had learned thirty words in Spanish and ridden some wonderful horses. I respectfully submitted my resignation and thanked the Chedraui's for the good rides and their great hospitality. It was time to say adios to the land of the jalapeno.

PART II

TRANSFORMATION

I fly to West Palm to spend Easter with Alice and William and enjoy some time near the ocean. Sandra Burgess gives me a well-worn copy of Patanjali's Sutras; it is a thought provoking read all about clearing the minefields on the road to the center of consciousness The goal is being able to witness thoughts in the mind without being disturbed by them. The teachings are sprinkled with Yogic aphorisms. "Live each moment completely and the future will take care of itself." Well I had been living that way and it worked for a long time… until it didn't. Running out of money in Switzerland and the pressures in Mexico were taking a toll. Suddenly the future is not what it was or is this just a thought?

The Sutras speak to the quality of life. The quantity seems to be prearranged; most people have four score years or something close to it. It is the quality that I need to get a handle on. When Sandra mentions that Yogi Amrit Desai is speaking at the Unity Church on Flagler - we find ourselves in the front row. I have no idea of what transformation is or that one is about to happen.

Amrit radiates a vibrant energy as he explains how some people think that yoga is a set of postures or a religion. However, religion is based on faith while yoga is a science that supports an optimal life. He points out "most people are governed by their incessant repetitive thoughts and insatiable desires. But there is a deeper consciousness that is alive and lives in satisfaction."

"We think our moods are created by external conditions and associate our inner changes with outer events. Then we use all the means at our disposal to feel the way we want, clinging to objects that make our energy flow and pushing away things that depress us. When we don't pay attention, our experience becomes chaotic. If we pay attention, we can see that all our decisions are based on the flow of energy and our moods are an internal ride."

Attention there it is again, he is talking about *feel* but this time it's about watching the mind's journey.

Amrit quoted the *Bhagavad-Gita,* (a sacred text of ancient India) that compares the human mind to a team of wild horses running toward what they want and away from whatever frightens them. I perk up at the mention of horses. In the discussion that follows I relate how I had been riding those horses in Mexico jumping between the desire to win and the fear of losing. In the end I lost my enthusiasm.

Amrit raised his hand, "The season of failure is the best time for sowing the seeds of success." He bypassed the analytical overlay and got right to the point. "Yoga does for the mind and body what consistent training does for the horse. What you are riding for is the transformation of your energy, if riding itself was the source of the happiness it would always make everyone happy."

I remembered my unbridled enthusiasm for Dobbin; according to Amrit I was bringing my bliss with me and not following it. During the guided meditation, these words resonated with my intuition and I realized how riding worked. I thank Amrit for the insights, and receive an invitation to Kripalu in the Berkshires.

UNDERMOUNTAIN FARM

Inspired again and ready to go to work, I call Candace at Professional Equine Employment and she tells me about a trainer's job in Western Massachusetts. "Where exactly?" I asked. She says it is in the Berkshires. There was the Guru's invitation, and now this job had come along, synchronicity at work. So I drive the Interstate 95 from Florida to New England watching the flow of my energy.

Tjasa Sprague is a bright pillar of the community with a great smile. She has built Undermountain Farm on the road between Tanglewood and Lenox and it is three miles from Kripalu the largest Yoga Center in the country.

The Ashram residents were welcoming and we quickly devise a barter system, in return for teaching some of my new friends to ride, I attend yoga and meditation classes. At the Thursday evening satsangs Amrit talks about the Yoga of consciousness rooted in stillness, where emotions are in harmony with the needs of the moment. Kripalu Yoga had great appeal since I seldom experienced tranquility and my emotions aren't in harmony with anything.

There are a good many vegetarian meals, but soy isn't my favorite and when overdosed with tofu, some of us would go off for supper at Salerno's. One evening in the midst of a pepperoni pizza, the discussion turns to the history of yoga. Shoban relates that the practice began in the Indus valley five thousand years ago when the Rishis condensed their highest spiritual aspirations into the sacred texts. I remember that horses were domesticated in Eurasia some time in the same millennium. Yoga and Horsemanship are two of the world's oldest disciplines, going back some five thousand years.

After consuming his third beer, Ashvin mentions that our quality of life increases in direct proportion to our awareness in the moment and that the best rides probably happen when horse and rider are unified in a single field of consciousness. Sounds good to me. The conversation moves on to Hatha Yoga and I conclude that this practice would keep a rider balanced and supple.

Out of these discussions a Wednesday riding program evolves. Amrit and the residents have planted the seeds of Conscious Riding, now I want help from a professional gardener.

THE INNER GAME

W. Timothy Gallwey is a coach and master of the art of peak performance. In his best-selling book "The Inner Game of Tennis," he talks about the outer game of rules, regulations and techniques and the inner game, which involves quieting the mind and trusting the body to get on with the sport.

Gallwey's Inner Game could be a template for Conscious Riding and I want his help to jumpstart the course. I get Tim's phone from his publisher and before I lose my nerve, I call his home in California to ask for help. Tim is cordial on the phone and generous with his time when I arrive in Malibu. He agrees to let me spend a week taking tennis lessons, talking about horses and receiving insights into the Inner Game.

My first day on the court at the Malibu Tennis Club is a revelation. With my K-Mart racket, running shoes and cut-offs I feel like Huckleberry Finn at Wimbledon. Tim begins with an awareness drill. His first instructions are clear and precise: "All I want you to do is watch the ball and say 'bounce' when the ball lands, and 'hit' when it hits my racket."

He tapped the ball into the air a few times, let it bounce, and then hit it in the air again. I said, "bounce" when it touched the ground, and "hit" when it met his racket. When I'd figure out this part, he gives me some new instructions: "Now I'm going to hit the ball over the net toward you. Just say 'bounce' the instant the ball lands and 'hit' when you would have hit it. But just let it go by."

The first calls are a bit off, but after a dozen or so, my timing improves. I am feeling better about my K-Mart racket — perhaps I won't even have to use it.

"Now whenever you feel like it, let your racket swing and say 'hit' when the ball meets the strings." Tim started hitting some easy shots in my direction." I let two go by and then hit the third one back over the net. I get excited and my next three shots go into the net.

"Were your 'bounces' and 'hits' on the last three balls early or late?" Tim asked.

"I don't know. The pressure was on, and returning the ball was exciting."

"Let's forget the game and stay with the drill. Just watch the ball and see if your calls are early or late." Tim's patience has its limits. He starts hitting them over again and I realize I am saying "bounce" before the balls land and "hit" sometime after they leave my racket. He hits several more over, I calm down and my timing improves again.

In a few minutes I am returning the ball consistently with my forehand. Then Tim lobbed the ball high in the air. I remember being alarmed, looking up and calling out "bounce" in a loud voice, commanding the ball to come down.

"Why did you do that?" Tim asked.

Embarrassed, I told him I knew the ball was coming down, but wanted it to land quickly. In another five minutes things smooth out, and my 'bounce' and 'hit' calls are right on the money. I am hitting them over the net and having a good time. Then he starts hitting the ball to my backhand.

I am trying to keep the ball in play, so I start running around the backhand shots and returning them with my forehand. My footwork is awkward and so are the returns. "Why don't you use your backhand?" Tim isn't amused.

I start to explain that since things are going well, I don't want to change my swing.

"Keeping the ball in play is not the point. Is it?"

This was a rhetorical question and didn't require an answer, but I tried anyway. "I wasn't sure I could hit the ball with my backhand and I didn't want to appear awkward…"

"You couldn't be more awkward. You must realize the only interesting thing about your tennis at this moment is your backhand. I can help you with it, if you give me a chance."

I have to take up the 'bounce, hit' mantra once again as Tim directs his shots to my backhand. After watching several balls go by and getting my timing right, I begin to swing my racket. Lo and behold, the backhand shots go over the net and the ball stays in play. "Bounce, hit. Bounce, hit. Bounce, hit," I call out. I am getting into the rhythm.

At lunch he tells me about the process. "Words and rhythm have a calming effect on the nervous system, but there's more to it. 'Bounce, hit' requires paying attention to something that is actually happening — in this case, the flight of the ball. As the ball comes toward you, your body-mind mechanism makes adjustments to the instructions it sends to the muscles. These messages are non-verbal and too complex to put into words."

"What was the point of 'bounce, hit' while you were hitting the ball at the beginning of the exercise?"

"That was to give you some idea of how a tennis ball behaves on a court without the distraction of trying to hit it. This is fundamental in creating the picture."

"How come you didn't ask me to pay attention to your stroke?"

"When you are watching the ball's movement carefully and saying 'bounce, hit,' you can't help but see the stroke. Your eye takes the picture and your muscle memory develops it. You get the information without consciously thinking about it, and you don't get bogged down in a lot of verbal instructions."

Tim talked about the natural learning process that takes place when the mind quiets down. The trick, he said, was to give the ever-thinking mind something to hold its attention. Then the body is free to perform at its full potential. At the end of the week he gave me his final word of advice. "Your students are your laboratories. Remember to stay in a teaching mode."

Tim is a remarkable coach and a great inspiration. He provided some well-timed encouragement that moved my program along. When I return to Lenox, I experiment to find a technique analogous to 'bounce hit' which would engage the mind and give the body a chance to learn what works.

I practice breathing in and out following the horse's steps. 1-2-3-4 at the walk, 1-2 at the trot, and 1-2-3 at the canter. The intuitive right brain feels the motion and the left-brain counts out the strides and coordinates breathing. By giving the two sides of the brain small tasks suited to their specialties, the body is free to learn. The Inner Game is a giant step forward.

RIDING FROM FEAR TO THERE

Early one morning while I'm schooling a horse, a woman in a blue Buick drives over to the ring. She sits in her car watching intently. I ride over to say hello.

"Do you teach people to ride?" Marcia introduces herself nervously and doesn't wait for a reply. "I haven't ridden in thirty years and I wasn't very good to begin with. You might not enjoy teaching me."

I thought about Tim's words: "Remain in a teaching mode." Before I can say a word, Marcia goes on with her story. "My husband is taking me to the Lazy J for our thirtieth anniversary. It's a dude ranch in Arizona. We went there for our honeymoon. Al really enjoyed the trail rides; we had to take them twice a day. I wasn't much of a rider then - now I'm terrified."

"It's going to be all right, let's give it a try" I reassure her as I put my horse away and bring out Lucky Favor. Marcia hadn't exaggerated her dilemma; every cell in her body is on red alert. After much hesitation, she gets on Lucky and clings to the reins for dear life.

I just hold the horse and wait. The minutes roll by. Lucky stands like a statue at the mounting block. I begin to understand that this was more than a refresher course for Marcia. This is about her self-esteem and showing Al she can still ride the range after thirty years of married life.

"Do you want to let Lucky walk?" Perhaps we can move through the anxiety.

"Sure." She doesn't sound sure, but she can't sit there forever.

"Let's just walk around the ring. See if you can feel the motion and count the steps." I attach a lead rope to Lucky's bridle and he follows me into the arena. We walk along slowly and she doesn't say a word.

"Just close your eyes. I'm not going anywhere." She complies.

"Now keep breathing, feel the motion, and let me hear you count the steps. One, two, three, four, as you feel each hind leg coming forward. This will take your mind off your fears."

When I look around, her eyes are wide open. The next time they are closed. "How does that feel?"

"Feels fine." Marcia smiles. "But I'm still scared."

"What are you really afraid of?"

"I'm afraid of lots of things: thunder and lightning, driving in the snow. Especially if my husband is behind the wheel. I'm afraid of skiing, but I do it anyway."

"Do you think this could be free-floating anxiety?"

"No, this doesn't feel free or floating. I have a real sense of being out of control. I could fall off, and who knows what would happen?"

I tried to simplify things. "So, is it a control issue?"

"Partly lack of control and then there is the fear of getting hurt. I remember a cowboy at the Lazy J telling me I had to be kicked, bitten and stepped on three times before I learned to ride."

I dispelled that myth and assured her that Lucky wasn't inclined to kick, bite or step on people. I also tell Marcia that the horse can't display these vices while she is in the saddle.

"My last ride at the Lazy J was terrifying. The horse in front of us kicked out and almost got us. I yelled for help, grabbed the saddle horn and dropped the reins. Old Lightning started to run and the whole group stampeded. The wrangler was furious. He said I scared the horses."

"Were you hurt?"

"No, just frightened, but I can't forget it. I know the only way to get rid of the fear is to ride again, but when I lose control I panic."

I told her horses have the same problem. "When you yelled, Old Lightning's fear got activated and he took off. Horses are sensitive to sounds and body language. We have to override our obstacles."

"What obstacles?"

"Stressful events create blocks. We let enjoyment flow right through, but we resist unpleasant situations and try to keep them away. Our resistance becomes an obstacle."

"What can I do about it?"

"You can learn to work with your fears."

Marcia looked distracted and shook her head.

"We're all afraid of the unknown and our imagination takes over."

Marcia could see that Lucky was cooperating and I was right there leading him around the arena. But she was worried about the next stampede.

So we went over her worries: driving, skiing and riding at the Lazy J. All the while Lucky walked along quietly. At one point Marcia acknowledged that her anxiety was probably greater than anything the horse intended. Riding Lucky and talking about things helps, but the ghosts were still there. It was almost one o'clock and my thoughts were heading toward lunch.

"What do you do when you get hungry?" I asked.

Marcia became animated; evidently she had no fear of food. "I find something in the fridge or make a quick stop for some fast food. Sometimes Al takes me to his favorite steak house, but I don't eat beef, I always have the chicken."

Marcia always tried to keep the peace. "What if you don't have time to eat?"

She sat up and took a deep breath. "I put my hunger on hold. I can eat later."

This was a breakthrough. "Either you eat or you put your appetite on hold. But you don't go into a feeding frenzy. When you want nourishment you crave food, and when you sense danger you want security."

I suggest that Marcia can deal with fear as easily as she dealt with hunger. "If you let go of the stampede memories, you can attend to what's happening here and now."

"You mean put my fear on hold, like my hunger?"

"Yes. Let's put some perspective on your anxiety. On a scale of zero to ten — zero is no fear at all and ten means you're petrified — how would your rate your fear? Don't think about it, just give me a number."

"Seven," she answers.

"Now let's get back to your body awareness. The walk is a four-beat gait. Count the horse's steps as you feel them and coordinate your breath." Lucky kept walking while Marcia did the exercise.

"Where is your fear now?"

"Five."

I ask Marcia if she would ride without the lead, while I walk close by.

"I remember Lightning used to pull on the reins and pick up speed. Now my fear is going back to seven." She hunches her shoulders and leans forward.

I asked her to move her attention from Lightning to Lucky. Then I encouraged her to stay with the motion and the breathing. She sits up and takes a deep breath.

"Which do you lose first, your control or your balance?"

Marcia shifts in the saddle and thinks about this for a moment. "My balance goes first. The control is mostly in my mind, but the balance is in my body."

"If you realign your position you'll regain your balance and control. If the horse picks up speed you'll fall back. If he stops suddenly you'll go forward. You would have the same experience on a roller coaster. As your coordination improves your body will realign automatically."

"I hear the instructions and repeat them to myself, but my body doesn't listen. When I can't follow instructions, I feel stupid."

"Stay with the motion, don't judge yourself. Don't think too much. Before you try a new position, check out your present alignment. You can't get where you're going if you don't know where you are."

"That's not easy to follow."

"If I call up and ask directions to your house, what's your first question?"

"Where are you?"

"Right, you have to know where I am before you can give me useful instructions. It's the same with riding a horse. You have to be aware of your position before you can change it."

Marcia shook her head. "If only I could make myself see what I am doing."

"Force creates resistance. You can't make yourself see. You need to let yourself see."

"I see." Marcia laughs for the first time this morning. The energy shifts. She still has bouts of anxiety, but they don't last long. After a dozen lessons, Marcia and Al celebrate their anniversary at the Lazy J.

Outdoor & Fitness

Performing any action consciously—fully aware of body, breath and environment—is a powerful and transformative practice. Done in this spirit, physical activity has the potential to change your entire outlook on life. And it's fun! Kripalu offers a range of invigorating options to promote wellness and vitality, all in our exquisite mountain setting.

Paul Striberry

Conscious Riding
Paul Striberry
Sept 6–8 • Sept 13–15
$270 tuition + 2 nights room & meals
Sept 19–22 • Sept 26–29
$390 tuition + 3 nights room & meals
Level: All

Conscious Riding employs yogic and meditative approaches to accelerate learning and increase the enjoyment of equitation. Riders are reminded that a horse can feel a fly land on his back so the horse's sensitivity is seen in a new light, and the result is equine equilibrium. "The horse is a spiritual utility vehicle, transporting the rider into the present moment of now," says Paul Striberry.

Riding takes place three miles from Kripalu at Undermountain Farm. The program includes two hours of riding a day and can include aspects of dressage and trail riding. Class size is limited.

NOTE: TUITION INCLUDES RIDING FEES. BRING GLOVES, BOOTS WITH HEELS AND A HELMET, IF YOU HAVE ONE.

Paul Striberry, a life member of the American Horse Show Association and an active member of the U.S. Combined Training Association, is a lifelong professional horseman.

REGISTER BY PHONE: 800-741-7353 / ONLINE: www.kripalu.org

CONSOLIDATING CONSCIOUS RIDING

Kripalu asked me for a course description with some idea of what the program will cover. Conscious Riding is all about performing on the leading edge of our own skill and the horse's ability. On this threshold we are fully alive and free from the distractions of time and the ego.

Nevertheless some rides go better than others. Even with first-rate instruction and painstaking practice many riders are discouraged when they don't fulfill their aspirations. Saturday morning the jumping goes well, next week same horse, same course and there are run outs or refusals. We certainly know the instructions but don't always follow them and it isn't that we don't try hard enough; we're often trying too hard. How many times must we be told to 'keep our leg on, and maintain contact through the reins? And how come sometimes it works and sometimes it doesn't?

The answers can be found in the conversation between horse and rider. A horse can feel a fly on his back, so every move can send him a message. Communicating through our legs, seat and hands and staying in touch with the horse's responses we will acquire *feel* (once thought to be the exclusive gift of elite horsemen). Feel is a skill set available to everyone; it boils down to having clear realistic goals, paying attention, timing and training our responses to become reflexes. Remaining conscious of these interconnected mental skills will create the optimal ride.

Well-defined goals are important, if we don't know exactly what we want, we may not want what we get. Goals are the beacons of our imagination; they focus our energy, provide motivation and suspend our neurotic preoccupations with life.

When long-term goals are broken down into short-term challenges, such as trying a new horse or jumping a new course, each achievement affords the satisfaction that keeps us on track. Riding satisfies our evolutionary urge to overcome fear and this requires leaving our comfort zone. While we are out, our vulnerabilities soon become strengths and the zone expands.

Attention is the medium that holds information in consciousness. The loss of attention is an early sign of losing control. During my clinics I can always spot the attentive riders; they notice and immediately correct the slightest drift off the rail. Others don't seem to see a problem until they are stuck in the middle of the ring with their horse chewing on a jump standard. Remaining alert enables well timed corrections - before the ride gets completely out of hand.

Our timing improves the same way that people getting faster at video games. Players and riders receive immediate feedback and positive reinforcement for getting it right. Whether it's the World of War Craft or our first competition, winning depends on remaining in the process and staying in the *now*. This concentration contracts time into present moment awareness, time is experienced in smaller increments and we seem to have more of it.

Our responses become reflexes when we train with focus, determination and commitment. Without distractions and riding intuitively we call on the embodied reflexes encoded in our muscle memory.

Training works best when we see the world from the horse's point of view. Its not that he *shouldn't* be afraid of the mailbox - he is. Now is the time to stay in touch and give him a chance to get over himself. The horse telegraphs his intentions when we're paying attention; is he tensing to kick or drop a shoulder and spin? When we fail to keep the horse's attention he will often find reasons to shy, other horses to engage or vegetation to eat. That's who he is and there is no point in blaming him.

An ego-involved rider will take the reactions personally and get angry. This confirms the horse's worst fears; punishment doesn't work because he has only a few seconds to associate cause and effect. Impatient reactions stimulate the flow of cortisol that makes it harder for horses to learn and store information. And most importantly we don't want them afraid to fail.

Task oriented riders maintain present moment awareness. They can control their minds and focus their attention at will, concentrating as long as necessary to achieve their goals. They work on improving their communication because they understand that the horse has to *get it* before he can *do it*.

A little bit of well-timed encouragement tells the horse there's something in it for him. Any inclination to *try* is quickly rewarded and a prompt release of the aids creates a flow of endorphins, which increases his willingness to please us. On the other hand, the slightest aggression or efforts to tune out the rider are quickly followed by *slowly* turning up the pressure of our aids. In time the horse learns to predict the rider's reactions.

Whenever we get on a horse our attitude and underlying emotions gets mixed up with his energy. Stress dulls our ability to feel and anxiety makes us react emotionally. The good news is we can influence the success of the ride by learning to watch our emotions without getting caught in them.

Researchers have shown that mindful meditation enhances brain connectivity, which improves our mental health and happiness. Even with all the well-established benefits many of us are not ready, willing or able to sit still for twenty minutes of just being. We are much more comfortable doing something – sometimes anything. So for the restless among us Conscious Riding offers meditation in motion.

Horses are the Spiritual Utility Vehicles and guides in this practice. They embody the ancient wisdom to 'Keep the mind alive and free.' The horse lives in the present moment and is fully engaged with reality. Ridden mindfully he can bring us back from disappointments in the past and retrieve us from our fears of the future.

There's a revitalizing connection between the ancients arts yoga and horsemanship. Hatha Yoga increases the integrity of the tendons and muscles that maintain our alignment; and riders are the perfect candidates. Many of us think we need to be flexible to begin the practice, however the less flexible we are the more there is to gain. After overcoming our the initial resistance we will begin to look forward to the stretching and bending which strengthens our position in the saddle and decreases the stress we put the horse.

The first few minutes warming-up is an excellent time to establish your foundation. Feel your seat bones following the movement at the walk and follow the motion of the horse's head and neck through the reins. Synchronize with the feeling of the hind legs stepping forward, notice the moment when each hind leg has pushed off and is in the air.

Find the rhythm and coordinate inhaling for four steps and exhaling for four. The right brain feels the motion and the left-brain counts the strides Concentration is easy since the steps provide an external focus, like the metronome for a pianist.

Take your time inhale deeply, breathing circulates your energy and is your connection to the present moment. Begin to notice how inhaling uplifts your position and exhaling softens it. As your breath becomes regulated, your pulse and respiration slow down and you can feel the horse relax.

When we are quiet and attentive we intuitively adjust to the horse's movements – which is essentially how we learn. Every gait has a rhythm and the challenge is responding to the changing tempos, now riding becomes a Zen experience of perpetual spontaneity.

Riding a challenging horse, we may be distracted by anxious thoughts and self-critical dialog. 'I'll never be able to do this, I'm making a fool of myself, I'm going to get hurt…' Most self-doubts have little basis in reality – they are born in fear and with repetition become part of our belief system.

When anxiety strikes it is important to realize the horse is not the cause of our distress, he is an ally and not the opponent, our agitated mind is the source of our feelings. Fear comes from worrying about what *might* happen in the future but the most important step is one we're taking now.

The Yoga of meditation is learning to watch our thoughts. Mindfulness enhances the mind's strength and improves its flexibility. If the mind is elsewhere we don't see what is right in front of us, we do not feel the ride. When the mind ceases its agitation, distractions end. It's not how often our attention wanders off, it's how quickly we bring it back that matters. When you lose it just smile and direct your attention back, the way you would quietly return a horse to the rail.

When we can control our mind we are free to get in touch with the part of our self that is inseparable from the horse.

THE WEEKEND COURSE

The chairs are arranged in a circle as the weekend program commences on Friday evening. We begin with a silent meditation, during which time I routinely notice that I am still addicted to my thinking, attracted to my emotions and can't sit quietly for more than a minute. My bumper sticker says 'I'd rather be riding.'

Getting acquainted, guests talk about their experience, and what they want to achieve. Each program brings riders of varied abilities — some with years of experience and others with fresh aspirations. The last weekend in September I had four students who posed some noteworthy questions.

Rod arrived a little late and out of breath, he introduced himself first, "I'm a psychiatrist, and I enjoy the quiet space around horses. The rest of my life is a wall of noise. I speak with patients all day and when I get home my wife and three daughters are talking non-stop. I started riding six months ago. I've taken twenty-four lessons and have fallen off six times."

"Six falls, in twenty-four…?" I passed the liability releases around the table for everyone to sign. "Don't these falls bother you?"

"At first they did, but now I have more respect for the horse and I've discovered a new resiliency."

I am impressed by his determination, but concerned for his life and limbs.

Ellen just left her job as a buyer for Bloomingdales, she had ridden on and off for years. She enjoyed buying new boots and wanted to buy a horse. "I grew up out west - riding with the cowboys and now I want to try an English saddle. I've gone to Monty Roberts' clinics and Equine-assisted Therapy sessions. It was interesting but we never rode. I need to get out of the round pen and work on my core issues."

"What are your issues?"

"My problem is my work ethic. I have been working hard for a long time and it doesn't get me anywhere. My other issue is that my grandfather died on a horse, I have an underlying fear that horses are dangerous."

I assured Ellen that she could work on these ideas.

"Monty said I was incongruent, my aids were clashing and sending the horse mixed messages. Do you teach anything about clashing aids?"

"This a common problem, when your ego wants to canter and your body wants to walk, you may ask for the canter and lose your balance. If you hold on with the reins you're saying stop. This eventually erodes the horse's good will."

"How do I get beyond the clashing?"

"Alignment and control will help."

Jim was an anchorman for a local TV station. He talked about the joys of cantering through the woods and jumping logs. "Of course, these are my plans. I've had four lessons in Rock Creek Park. I want to ride for fun but I'm not there yet."

"How did you become a newscaster?" I assumed if he could anchor the broadcast he could learn to ride a horse.

Jim gave a prime-time smile. "I started my career reading the papers and reporting stories at dinner. The family was very patient, although if my brother had read the Daily News, he would correct my facts. When I started watching the six o'clock report, I added some style to my reports. Watching and copying worked for me."

His talent for observation might serve him well on a horse.

Julia is in her early thirties, the youngest but most seasoned rider in the group. "I've ridden all my life. Cantering takes me back to the swings in the playground. I have a Thoroughbred, I'm OK when he's cantering slowly, but frightened when I lose control."

"What are we going to do this weekend?" Rod just wants the facts.

"This evening, we'll explore equine equilibrium. Saturday morning we work on the basics in the arena. If all goes well we'll go out on the trail. Saturday afternoon we ride bareback and then meet back here to discuss what you've learned, what you still have to learn, and what's holding you back. Sunday morning we'll try some jumping and put it all together."

"Could you explain equine equilibrium?" Ellen is tilting back precariously on the legs of her chair.

"It's the balanced 'can-do' feeling when body and mind are fully engaged with the horse."

"How do we access this equilibrium?"

"Don't think too much or try too hard. In a way, it's like sleep. You can't make yourself fall asleep, it overtakes you in its own time."

"Is there a shortcut? " Rod could hardly wait.

"Focus on the means, not the end. Riding is a kinesthetic experience that only happens in the here and now. The shortcut is feeling more and thinking less."

"Can I learn riding the way I learned tennis?" Rod had won several tournaments.

"Riding is a game without a competitor. When people are concerned with winning, they give away their power; they become dependent on one horse or one trainer. When they don't get ribbons they look for a new horse or another trainer. The search exhausts their resources, eventually they may look inside."

"You mean the ability is within?" Jim wasn't sure.

"Where else could it be? Learning requires intention, attention and the will to practice. The details fall in place when you chose pay attention."

"How does choice come into it?"

"Thoughts come and go at random, but you can decide where to pay attention."

"Can we choose emotions?" asked Julia.

"The ordinary rider experiences an emotional state and acts it out. If she feels anger she may punish the horse. The conscious rider will watch her anger but not let it take over. The horse takes the rider's emotions to the next level, either getting excited or calming down."

"Why is it so difficult to learn to ride?"

"The horse has power, speed and a mind of his own and we have to learn self control before we can control him. Green horses and new riders must trust the unknown."

"My eight-year-old daughter is fearless. Why do children learn faster?" Ellen was looking for confidence.

"Children learn to walk before they learn to talk. They experiment with gravity and make intuitive adjustments and that's also how we learn to ride."

"How can we get back there?"

"Progress comes from making the shift from the mind's narrow thinking to the body's present moment awareness."

"Why is it so hard to stay in the present?" Julia asked.

"Time travel starts early. Children are required to sit in school learning by rote rather then experience. They study the past to pass tests in the future; they're rewarded for a good memory and discouraged from being spontaneous. As adults we are inundated by media, so we disassociate from our bodies and avoid life as it happens."

"This may seem strange, but when is now?"

"It is always now although the present lasts about three seconds. Now is when you pay attention to what is actually happening. The past and future are just thoughts, they only exist when you think about them. The present is unique, alive and illuminated."

"Do horses know when we're afraid?" Jim looks worried.

"Horses are prey animals. They survive in nature by watching and listening for predators. Their ability to pick up on the fear of another is a lifesaving skill. But you can build confidence by treating them as partners instead of possessions. Remember to thank him; you won't feel gratitude and fear at the same time.

THANKING DUNRAVEN AT MILLBROOK

"How long does this take and what can I expect tomorrow?" Rod was speeding around the learning curve.

"Expect the experience you'd like to have, how fast you progress depends on your coordination and conditioning."

"Are there techniques we can practice to be in the moment?"

"While you walk, breathe in for four steps and out for four. This will focus you in the here and now. As you're resting breathe in rhythm with your heartbeat."

Visualization can help; draw on the images in your mind to focus your consciousness. The trick is to first picture, then feel and enjoy the ride you want. The more elements you bring to your imagination, the better the results. You can write, produce and direct a high definition video of your ideal ride and inspire your dreams as you fall sleep.

THE FLYING HORSE MEDITATION
Close your eyes and summon your imagination.
You Cantering down a country lane in the bright sunshine
On a dapple-grey mare with wings.
The road is your life's path.
It began before you were born and never ends.
Your past winds away behind you, as you ride through time.
There are green valleys and tree-covered hills in the distance.
Now Pegasus lifts off into the sky.
The countryside is spread beneath you.
Your life's path takes on a new perspective.
The higher you go the more you survey.
Looking down you can see the green hills.
The rivers that carried you along.
The swamps that bogged you down.
And the paths that vanished in the night.
From up here you can see your early goals and aspirations.
Your childhood dreams, making the team, your first real job.
They really weren't destinations, but signposts - To where?
Each goal was just another stepping-stone.
A trail shrouded in mist stretches into the future.
The road continues, as you fly on.
Fix your eyes on the opportunities ahead.
A bright future is created by your desires.
The sun is setting now. Darkness gathers.
Look around the night sky. Observe the constellations.
Realize you are never alone or helpless.
The power that guides the stars guides your life as well.
Your winged horse is drifting back to earth.
After the journey you always return to the present moment.
The best of times is the here and now.

**SATURDAY MORNING
OUT OF YOUR MIND — INTO YOUR BODY
ONTO THE HORSE**

Some of the guests like to groom and saddle their horses so I get to the barn early. Once they mount I adjust their stirrups and check that their reins are short enough to maintain control and long enough to keep the horse comfortable.

Ellen mounts first; she wears a new hunt cap, new boots, and everything new in between. Domino's coat matches her outfit.

Julia wears jeans and well-worn chaps. She spends a moment greeting Grigio, mounts and they walk easily off to the ring.

Jim is tense but smiling and Brewster starts moving sideways.

"This horse makes me nervous." Jim says, stepping out of the way. Giving him instructions is better than pointing out that he is making the horse nervous.

"Relax, exhale and take a moment to check your girth."

63

Jim gets on with a winning smile, a straight back and square shoulders. Brewster can't see the smile; he only feels the tension and walks ahead quickly.

Rod practically vaults on to Greylock startling the small Thoroughbred, she starts tossing her head and wringing her tail. "What did I do to deserve this?" He asks impatiently.

"When you calm down the horse will too."

"This isn't working," Rod exclaims as Greylock knocks over a jump standard. He gets off before the mare stops. Can you make her settle down?"

I take the reins and mount, Greylock quietly walks, trots and canters in both directions.

"Guess it must be me, can I get back on?"

"When you rush, horses feel threatened and reacts accordingly. Everything the horse does you have either asked for or allowed."

I left the ring for a moment and returned riding Caspian.

"Don't instructors usually teach from the ground?" Ellen didn't want the lifeguard to be surfing.

"It's demonstration, observation and repetition. Some things are skipped in the explanation, but when you watch you can take it all in.

I ask riders to pay attention as my horse steps each hind leg forward at the walk and notice how he overbalances himself with his head and neck and rebalances stepping forward with a front leg. Posting to the trot and I encourage them feel to how the horse's back provides the upward impulsion and gravity brings them down. Finally they watch the canter and take in the three beat rhythm.

"I'm happy walking, but cantering on a new horse worries me." Julia was getting tense.

"Take your time and watch your feelings. Confidence emerges with understanding."

"Why does this horse keep speeding up?" Ellen asks.
She is leaning forward on Domino's neck and he's accelerating.

"Its your position. What would it feel like if you leaned back?"

She sat up and let her shoulders relax.

"Speaking of position?" Jim was looking for the *right* spot.

"Remember, your position isn't static, when the horse moves you are going with him. Remain flexible and enjoy the effortless effort."

"I found my balance, but I'm out of breath." Julia inhaled.

"When you hold your breath, you lose it. Scan your body, find the tension and ask yourself: 'What emotion is holding on?' Emotions are the links between your mind and body."

"What is my horse trying to tell me?"

"Is he pulling on the reins? Perhaps you're holding them too tight. Are his ears back? Look for what is aggravating him; could it be your leg or the other horses?"

"It's a new language?" Rod knew several languages.

"The first time we ride, we hardly understand anything. We might as well be on a carousel. Our chattering minds and the instructions prevent us from really feeling the horse."

"How can I make this work?

"Make sure you're *on purpose* - if the horse doesn't know what you want, you may not want what you get. Horses left to their own devices wouldn't go around in circles for an hour. This isn't Disney World."

"Can we try the trot?"

"Sure. Get comfortable at the sitting trot, then expand your comfort zone and pick up posting. Shorten your reins and signal your horse. When he's alert, ask with your legs and yield with your hands." Brewster starts to trot and Jim starts to bounce.

"This is uncomfortable, what should I do?"

"Slow down and the trot will smooth out."

"Why is Domino cutting the corners and heading for the gate?" Ellen was frustrated.

"You're letting the horse take the path of least resistance. When you overcome your own inertia the horse will work for you."

"How do you make it look easy?"

"Try not to try too hard. When you get on, give the horse some space to get comfortable. Gradually you'll establish a relationship and then ask for a response, if he complies ease off and let him know he's doing it right."

"I want to canter but I'm stuck?" Ellen was stuck in her thoughts.

"Check the timing and pressure of your aids. Sit up, inhale and collect your energy. Get your horse's attention and creates some impulsion. Place your outside leg behind the girth and swing into the canter. If it doesn't work halt and repeat the process until it does. Remember to ride the question into the answer."

"It might easier to canter on the trail." Ellen liked the wide-open spaces.

I agreed. "A change of scenery perks up the horses.

Thinking that Ellen might have trouble with Domino on the trail, I brought out Falstaff and asked her to ride the quiet quarter horse instead. She wasn't thrilled with the change, but she did want to ride out.

On the way back we stopped in a hayfield. Julia was cantering in circles when three deer ran by; her horse shied and galloped around at a good clip. She made no effort to stop and Grigio kept going faster. Julia didn't respond to instructions, but Caspian was a steady horse, so I moved into their path and they came to a halt.

Julia was upset with her horse and herself. I asked about her lack of control, but she wasn't ready to talk about it and we rode back to the stable without further incident.

After lunch we are in the indoor ring to ride bareback. Emma is a Morgan mare with comfortable gaits and a mind of her own.

Ellen decides to go first. "How do I do this?"

"Place yourself behind the horse's center of gravity, sit up and you'll find the right spot." She tentatively mounts and Emma begins walking in a circle. Ellen is still thinking while the horse walks into the center and stops.

"What should I do now?"

"You can either stand there or ride out on the circle. It's up to you." Ellen gets the point and rides Emma out. They walk for a while do some trotting and the horse wanders in again.

"What's supposed to happen?"

"Notice what you're feeling when the horse stands still and when she walks and trots.

"What if I can't feel it?"

"The feelings are there. Relax and feel them." Ellen doesn't say anything; Emma walks out to the circle and trots around a few more times.

Rod is next. I lead Emma over, he jumps on and she trots off. Normally the horse has an easy trot, but Rod gets off to a rough start.

"Can I try cantering?"

I thought he might walk first, but I'll let him have the ride he wants.

"What should I do?"

"Stop bouncing, inhale and swing into the canter." Rod must have spent some quality time on the swings, because Emma easily canters off.

"And walk – whoa." Emma picks up my cue and comes down to a quiet walk. Rod dismounts smiling.

Jim is reluctant to ride without a saddle. Then without hesitation he gets on and sits very still. The horse walks off and then suddenly stops, raises her head and lays back her ears

"This isn't working."

"Actually it is. You are sitting still and the horse is standing there."

"Aren't we supposed to be going in a circle?"

"If you want to walk, move the horse on with your leg and open the door with the reins."

"How do I know when I'm ready to trot?"

"Emma will tell you. If you're not ready the horse won't trot."

Julia is the last to ride; she has ridden bareback and is comfortable. When she begins to lose her balance she resists the temptation to overcorrect. She asks for the canter and the horse steps directly into it.

Back in the solarium it is interesting to note how each rider's mindset affected the ride. It is time to review what they learned, what they want to learn on Sunday and what's holding them back.

Ellen complained, "My feelings were hurt when I had to ride Falstaff"

"Sorry. It was about safety. Domino might have run off on the trail."

"I'm not buying that…"

"You're shopping for instructions but you're not following them."

"But I'm trying,"

"Let's take trying out of the equation. We'll just leave doing and not doing as options."

"I'm confused," Ellen leans forward as she had on Domino.

"Try to pick up the pen on the table."

Ellen picked it up.

"No that's picking it up. Just *try*."

She is still leaning forward in her confused position.

"Trying is procrastination. Either you pick it up or you don't."

"You've nailed it." Ellen's face lit up and her back straightened. "Whenever life's not working - I go shopping. I buy all these self-improvement tapes and I listen intently but never follow the instructions. Shopping is my lifestyle."

Julia was struggling. "I know what I need to do, but anxiety is stopping me."

"Fear is about what might happen in the future. When you get on a horse and the unexpected happens, (as you can expect it will) anticipation turns to apprehension."

"How can I stay in the moment? My fear increases with speed."

" Your past is only a collection of thoughts; you don't have to keep thinking them. What was going on when Grigio galloped off this morning? The ride got out of control in a hurry. You ride well enough to keep that horse together. Has this happened before?"

Julia sighed. "Yes, I remember the riding school when I was fourteen. We had a few weeks of instruction, and then there was a horse show with all the students. I was riding Trinket when the judge called for a canter. A car backfired and we were galloping around the ring. The announcer was shouting, the judge scattered, I jumped off and the whole thing was over."

"When you disassociate you go blank and leave the decisions up to a frazzled horse. When it comes down to effective riding – you must be present to win."

"Do you remember what happened before you lost control?"

"No" she was starting to cry. "But when I get scared I lose it."

Then Julia recounted being abused as child and how she coped by giving up control and disassociating from the experience.

Everyone was quiet for a moment. By telling the story, Julia realized how her unresolved emotional experience blocked her energy under stress. Talking about the trauma freed her resolve; she was ready to stay in control.

"I think I'm afraid of fear," Jim announced

"The trick is watching your fear, but not getting involved, pretend you are watching an old scary movie."

"Why does this fear show up when I'm riding?"

"You bring it with you to the mounting block. Fight or flight energy turns to anxiety if it isn't used for fighting or fleeing.

"But fear is a strong emotion."

"When we put words around sensations they become emotions and when we put words around our emotions they become our stories. Our emotions determine our perception, if I'm in a good mood and my horse jumps around, I'll take in stride. If I'm in a bad mood, I might take a dim view of his antics.

"I don't know what I'm really afraid of?"

"If you're worried about getting hurt, perhaps you're moving too fast. If the challenge is getting ahead of your skill set, slow down. Of course fear of failure is an ego game. The ego is a self-perpetuating attention getting device that siphons off our energy. It's always waiting to play ego games, but you don't have to play with it."

"Can a fear always be identified?"

"Ask yourself some questions. Have I felt this fear before? What do I really think is going to happen? Don't always go with the first answer. Give the process a chance, if you ask the right question the answer will appear."

Jim is quiet for a moment, "I'm catching on. The news at dinner wasn't the whole story. Sometimes I was afraid there wasn't enough food to go around and I took it upon myself to eat last, waiting to see that everyone else had enough. When I was quiet my mother noticed, but the news was a distraction. Broadcasting was my hope for the future. It would mean success and enough of everything. Some part of me is still stuck in this poverty consciousness and I don't want to get into those fears."

"Maybe it's time to let go of the past."

Jim looked relieved. Brewster had inspired some soul searching.

"I want to learn quickly, but it's not happening." Rod was still talking fast.

"Your riding did improve this morning, perhaps your expectations are out of sync."

"I want to gallop." Rod was confusing learning quickly with going fast.

"Your ego wants to gallop. Your body is telling you to take your time.

"How fast do horses go?"

"They walk at four miles per hour. The trot ranges from six to eight. The canter is from eight to twelve. Racehorses go twice that speed. What you're looking for is a steady rhythm, don't outrun your ability to feel it."

"So being in a hurry isn't going to work." Rod took a deep breath.

"Wanting to learn 'right now' adds a lot of stress. How long have you been in a hurry?"

"I've rushed all my life. My father was a doctor in the Army. We moved from country to country every few years. I was always changing schools and starting over. I took accelerated programs in college and medical school so I could settle down and live in one place. But I'm still on the run. I see too many patients and play a fast game of tennis to unwind after work. My tennis coach tells me to slow down but I still charge the net." Rod wasn't in a hurry to slow down.

"You can rush through life to get to the end or take your time and enjoy the ride."

"Do you ever have fear training horses?" Julia wanted to know she wasn't alone.

"Misgivings cross my mind from time to time. Last year I bought a three year old Hanoverian, she was big, athletic and easily startled. 'Daily' rekindled my childhood fears of failing, falling and looking foolish. Working in a round pen we began to bond. I got her saddled and bridled. In a week I could get on and ride, but it was rough. When the chickens told her 'the sky is falling' she would rear straight up like the Statue of Liberty."

"How did you deal with the fear?"

"Frustration turned out to be a road sign telling me when to back off. I had bitten off more than I could chew, but I was determined to swallow it. The fear of failure was stronger than the fear of getting hurt; sometimes my ego creeps into the process."

"What happened with Daily?"

"I slowed down, lowered my expectations and spent a lot of quiet time developing trust and respect. Eventually I sold her to a breeder in Texas."

"Sometimes I can put it all together." Rod was catching on. "But then it's gone."

"Change is part of learning, the only thing you can maintain is your attention."

"How can I tackle my fear?" Ellen asked.

"Don't call it fear - just notice sensations as they appear. Is it raw adrenaline coursing through your veins? Perhaps you are seeing pictures of old accidents or imagining new ones. Turn off those programs and visualize the ride you want."

"What happens when you lose it?" Julia asked

"I have fallen and gone off course more times than I care to remember. My problems were always caused by insufficient preparation. Did I walk the course enough to remember it under pressure? Was the horse schooled adequately? Did I enter him in a class that was over his head? The answers were lessons I had to learn.

SOMETIMES YOU LOSE IT

"I hate making mistakes." Jim seldom made a mistake on TV.

"Losing your balance isn't a mistake, its just information from your body's positioning system that tells you to realign.

"I'm still feeling nervous." Julia spoke cautiously. "What if I have an accident?"

"Just call it a learning experience. Accidents happen—and you survived all the previous ones. Riding is a risk exercise sport, that's part of what keeps you coming back."

"And you say anyone can achieve equanimity?" Rod wanted it all in one piece.

"Equanimity is a state of mind not a set of circumstances. In the present moment there are no problems; only situations that engage your energy and call up your best instincts."

"How do I know what my horse is thinking?"

"You can get a clue from his body language. When a horse is holding his head high, he is working off his surroundings and one step away from flight. When he lowers his head and rounds his back he is usually amenable to the aids."

"How can I encourage my courage?"

"Look for the value. Think of the rodeo riders – and their calculated risks. The cowboy's life and fortune depend on riding an eight second round. In the chute, he slides down easy on the horse's back, takes the rope in one hand and tugs the brim of his hat with the other. The gate swings open and 'Thunder' leaps into the arena.

"Horses buck with different styles, some rear and plunge, some gallop and spin. But the winning cowboy stays loose and centered. He'll have one arm waving in the air, his legs spurring from shoulder to flank in perpetual motion. The contest is won by staying in the moment. Fears and dreams are put aside and pain is on hold. All that remains is riding the horse the way he's going and transforming eight seconds into the eternal now."

"What if we're not the rodeo type?" Ellen avoided the rodeos.

"Then there are other kinds of courage. One Friday evening a woman arrived with a Seeing Eye Golden Retriever. Cathy explained she had a pinpoint of vision; something like looking at the world through a straw. She had ridden for years until a car accident resulted in her blindness. She listened to the first night's proceedings. On Saturday she rode and did all the training exercises - everyone forgot she was blind.

"On Sunday she wanted to jump some fences. I let her start over the cross rails. In fact, she was jumping so well that I asked two other riders to follow her over the rails. As she went around the ring Cathy turned and remarked, "look at those dummies following the blind person."

She could focus on the jumps, but she really couldn't see the fence around the arena. Fortunately the horse took care of that part. I'll never forget her courage, sense of humor and the inspiration she provided."

Sunday morning Ellen rode Domino, this time she bought the ride. I asked her to demonstrate hunching up in the saddle and then sitting up and relaxing. When she sat up Domino moved forward with good impulsion. She guided the horse away from the gate and out on the rail. "Do you have more exercises for staying present?"

"Remember the present moment is not an abstraction it is a tangible reality. Cantering through around listen to your horse's hooves hitting the ground, feeling the motion all through your body. When you are immersed in any of your senses you are fully present."

"Then attention, awareness and consciousness work together" Jim was getting it.

"Paying attention is what you do. Awareness is what you get and consciousness is the source."

"The source of what?"

"The source of everything. Consciousness is alive, eternal and evolving. Some people call it the universal energy or the ground of being."

"Talking about staying conscious, why do riders take chances?" Julia's anxiety was subsiding.

"We have an evolutionary urge to overcome fear. When we get comfortable at the walk, we want to trot, and then canter. Next its horse shows, eventing or foxhunting. Upgrading our skills makes us feel fully alive."

"Can we risk cantering now?" Rod was ready.

"Sure! First get the horse's attention with a half halt, increase the contact of your legs and reins, but release the pressure before he stops. It's like testing your breaks. When the horse is alert, apply your outside leg behind the girth, release your rein and follow the motion."

"What if he doesn't respond?"

"Intensify your leg pressure and if necessary add the tap of your stick behind the saddle. As the horse takes the first step into the canter be sure to go with him."

"What if he does respond?" Ellen wasn't taking any chances.

"Just do it." She brought her lower leg back and tapped. Domino took two steps at the trot and broke into a smooth canter. After a brief hesitation Ellen flowed with the motion.

"What about jumping, are we ready to take the leap?" Rod wanted it all.

"If you can use your aids independently and maintain your position at the canter, you're ready."

"I'm worried." Jim imagined the horse jumping him out of the saddle, or refusing and throwing him over the fence. "What should I do?"

"Visualize a different program. See yourself effortlessly clear the fence. Stay flexible - the horse's motion will close your hip angles and put you in the right spot."

"How do I get to the fence?"

"Guide the horse straight to the middle of the cross rails with enough impulsion. Jumping is up to the horse; try not to interfere with his concentration. Once the horse leaves the ground maintain a firm leg and flexible back. When in doubt grab a handful of mane."

"How am I going to remember all of this?" Ellen wanted to work it out in her mind.

"Don't even try. If you want to give your mind a job count the strides as you approach the fence. This will keep your left-brain counting and your right-brain feeling. Keep your attention on the ride instead of the rules." Ellen cantered around and Domino jumped neatly over the fence.

THE LAST OBSTACLE

The four riders are lined up and cantering over the rails as I gradually raise the bar. Every jump isn't perfect but each effort is an improvement on the one before.

I think back to Friday night when Rod arrived out of breath and on the mark to race through the weekend. He works and plays in the express lane. Now he is slowing down and discovering that time is there to enjoy.

Ellen came all the way from Texas to window-shop. Domino was a bargain, his color matched but her disposition was off. Over the course of the weekend she heard the instructions but didn't listen. Then the light went on, and she got in touch with the horse, and now is jumping with a touch of the Wild West.

Jim sat still at his job and his position was static on the horse. Brewster finally shifted Jim's attention from the news to the actual story. Horse and rider were unified, under control and comfortable. The immobile anchor became a roving reporter.

On the trail ride Julia had up to relieve her stress. Now she knows that safety and control go together.

I remembered to my first lesson with Eunice and the crashing ladder that sent Drifter running off. Perhaps we're all a work in progress - riding through our fears of falling, failing and looking foolish.

DREAMS COME TRUE